FOR IAN CHARLESON

FOR
IAN CHARLESON

A Tribute

CONSTABLE · LONDON

First published in Great Britain 1990
by Constable and Company Limited
3 The Lanchesters, 162 Fulham Palace Road, London W6 9ER
Introduction © 1990 Ewen Maclachlan
The pieces are copyright respectively:
© 1990 Alan Bates, © 1990 David Puttnam,
© 1990 Hilton McRae, © 1990 Di Trevis,
© 1990 Hugh Hudson, © 1990 Elizabeth Charleson,
© 1990 David Rintoul, © 1990 Ruby Wax,
© 1990 Sharman Macdonald, © 1990 Richard Warwick,
© 1990 Johanna Kirby, © 1990 Peter Eyre, © 1990 John Whitworth,
© 1990 Sean Mathias, © 1990 Catriona Craig,
© 1990 Suzanne Bertish, © 1990 Kenneth Charleson,
© 1990 Richard Eyre, © 1990 Ian McKellen
ISBN 0 09 470250 0
Set in Linotron 11pt Sabon by
Rowland Phototypesetting Limited
Bury St Edmunds, Suffolk
Printed in Great Britain by
St Edmundsbury Press Limited
Bury St Edmunds, Suffolk

A CIP catalogue record for this book
is available from the British Library

I have wasted so much time
Time that was not mine to waste
And now I cry for that wasted
time and pull up my soul from
the dark cave in which I have
Kept it all this while
and I say . . . you are free

Ian Charleson, 1989

CONTENTS

ILLUSTRATIONS

Portrait, August 1989, by Johnny Rozsa

Cat on a Hot Tin Roof, National Theatre, 1989, photograph by
John Haynes

With Lindsay Duncan in *Cat on a Hot Tin Roof*, 1989,
photograph by John Haynes

In rehearsal, 1989, photograph by John Haynes

Portrait, 1988, by Johnny Rozsa

ACKNOWLEDGEMENTS

The publishers would like to thank Ian McKellen, Hilton McRae, Hudson Film Limited, Reg Wilson, John Haynes, Allied Stars, the press office of the Royal National Theatre, Twentieth Century Fox, Sean Mathias and Mr and Mrs Jack Charleson for their help and support with preparing this book for press.

Particular thanks go to Ewen Maclachlan for his work on the pieces by Ruby Wax, Suzanne Bertish, David Rintoul, Alan Bates and Hilton McRae.

The poem by John Whitworth and the piece by Richard Eyre were first published in the *Spectator* and *Guardian* respectively.

All royalties from the sale of this book will go to the Ian Charleson Fund.

INTRODUCTION

By Ewen Maclachlan

He was born on 11 August 1949 at the Eastern General Hospital in Edinburgh and given his father's name John Charleson. From birth, however, he was always called Ian, the Gaelic form of John. His father was a printer, his mother a housewife: both solid Scottish working people, good socialists. The family lived in a flat in a tenement building at Piershill, a grey and unlovely suburb, a couple of miles from the centre of Edinburgh. Later they would move to a house in the slightly more affluent suburb of Craigentinny. The Charlesons had one other child, Kenny, who was three when Ian was born and the family was completed eleven years later with the birth of a girl, Lizzie.

Ian's theatrical début was in *Princess Chrysanthemum*, a Sunday School entertainment, in which his performance as The Cat, wearing a costume made by his mother from old socks, was much admired. On the strength of it he was offered, at the age of nine, a part in *Kith and Kin*, a play performed by New Restalrig Church Dramatic Society. He played John, a child whose mother dies. Several of the audience were so moved by his performance that they wept.

His schooling began at the local primary, Parsons Green, where his teachers included Norman McCaig, the poet, who noticed Ian had an artistic nature. He was a quiet, happy boy who didn't like football or other sports. A bright child, too. At the age of eleven he won a scholarship to the Royal High School. Even in adult life he would be proud of this achievement.

The Royal High was an all boys, fee-paying school in the centre of Edinburgh. Not a public school but a school with tradition, it counted among its former pupils Sir Walter Scott and a Prince of Wales. Ian was happy there. 'Perhaps', he was to say later, 'I like institutionalized life.'

They played rugby at the Royal High which Ian liked even less than football. He was, he recalled, 'quite an erudite little chap, living in a complete dream world'. Science and maths baffled him. Art and music were his favourite subjects. He joined the school choir and, at the age of thirteen had his first press notice, the *Scotsman*'s critic observing that his soprano solo in Tippett's *Nunc Dimittis* was 'well sung'.

There was little scope for acting at the Royal High – few school plays and no drama classes – but Ian took any chances that he could. He played Young Marcius in his school's production of *Coriolanus* and later joined 'The Jasons', an amateur dramatic group. Neither of his parents had a taste for the theatre, though his mother had been a keen amateur singer and dancer in her youth, but they were proud of their son and went to all his performances. They would continue to do so throughout his life.

'My parents expected their children to be industrious and of high moral character,' Ian said, 'Oddly enough we turned out like that.' He became a school prefect and won first prize for art. When he had passed his Highers, he was accepted by Edinburgh University to study architecture.

He began his course in the autumn of 1967. The lectures, particularly those on Fine Art, were fascinating but he was weak at the more practical aspects of architecture. His models of buildings dripped glue and were covered in ink stains. In one exam he designed a magnificent bridge with no foundations.

Meanwhile he had plunged into the world of the university dramatic society. It was, he recalled later, a remarkably talented group. Several of his fellow DramSoc members would go on to careers in the professional theatre. Ian's first appearance was as Malvolio in *Twelfth Night*, to be followed by a string of equally good parts: Gaveston in *Edward II*; John Worthing in *The Importance of Being Earnest*; the psychiatrist in *What the Butler Saw*; Tony Lumpkin in *She Stoops To Conquer*; the herald in *Marat/Sade*. He was given singing parts as well. He designed costumes. He directed plays, including one at the Traverse Theatre. He became, according to the *Edinburgh Evening News*, 'a well-known figure in fringe circles'. In the chorus of praise for his performing talents, there was, he noted, nobody telling him he was destined for glory as an architect. By his second year he had decided to abandon architecture and settle for an MA in arts subjects. When his close friend David Rintoul was accepted by RADA, a new option opened up. A note in the programme of *She Stoops To Conquer* declared Ian's intent: 'After graduating next year Ian Charleson hopes to train for the professional theatre.'

LAMDA meant living away from home for the first time. Initially Ian found life tough in London. He lived in a bed-sit in Earls Court and missed his friends. That first year, he was to describe as, 'the loneliest ever for me. I encountered a lot of people but made no permanent friendships. It was my own fault. I thought the majority of people were inferior.' He was always hard up – a problem throughout his time at LAMDA for he had no student grant. He made some money singing in the evenings at the restaurant Food For Thought and later took a job clearing the tables at the newly-opened Hard Rock Café. This was more like fun since the Hard Rock was 'one of the grooviest places in London' and the customers included Richard Harris, Edward Fox, Julie Christie.

People were starting to notice him and invite him into a glamorous new world. Cherry Vanilla, one of Andy Warhol's 'stars', spotted him at the Hard Rock and invited him to parties. He was making theatre contacts, including Frank Dunlop, the director of the Young Vic. He loved his course at LAMDA, just as he had loved school and university. Teachers thought he was talented, though with a lot to learn. 'I'd been a very flashy and noisy actor,' he said. 'At LAMDA they taught me to do it from the inside. They kept saying "facility is not enough". So I got very introvert.' He played Christian in a version of *The Pilgrim's Progress* and, at the end of his second year, Ford in *The Merry Wives of Windsor*. By this time, though he had another year to go, he had decided to give up the struggle of surviving without a grant and leave LAMDA. He persuaded Frank Dunlop to watch his performance as Ford, and, a few days later, was offered small parts in the two productions the Young Vic were doing at the Edinburgh Festival, *A Comedy of Errors* and *Joseph and the Technicoloured Dreamcoat*.

Within a few months of leaving LAMDA, still with the Young Vic, he was playing Jimmy Porter in *Look Back In Anger* and Hamlet in *Rosencrantz and Guildenstern Are Dead*. In a review of *Rosencrantz and Guildenstern*, Michael Billington of the *Guardian* observed presciently: 'Ian Charleson's Scottish Hamlet convinces you he could easily sustain a five-act tragedy.' Other productions brought overseas tours and took Ian on the first of many visits to New York, a city which initially overwhelmed and alarmed him. 'During the Young Vic years,' Ian said, 'I was

[xvii]

finding my style as well as myself.' Having learnt at LAMDA to look inwards, he found that at the Young Vic, in those hectic, populist days, 'everyone else was way over the top'.

Appearances in television plays followed, and, in 1974, the thrilling opportunity to play Hamlet, at the age of twenty-four, in a touring production for the Cambridge Theatre Company. The *Glasgow Evening News* hailed him as 'a new star in the making', but, long before the end of the run, Ian was sick of the production and dissatisfied with his own performance. The role of Hamlet would remain on his agenda as unfinished business.

After Hamlet came his first West End part, a surly Scottish lodger in Simon Gray's *Otherwise Engaged*, directed by Harold Pinter with a real West End star, Alan Bates. Ian was on the huge salary of £100 a week, the critics liked the show and it ran for a year. Though the newspapers were still having difficulty identifying him – *The Times* printed a photograph of him captioned 'Julian Glover'; the *Scotsman*, in their review, called him Sam Chaulson – Ian loved the play and relished his part.

By now he had great number of friends and acquaintances in London, a mixture of old friends from Edinburgh and a newer, flamboyant circle. He thought London was a beautiful city. He liked parties and town life. But his habitual pleasures remained simple: playing the piano, playing cards and board games of all sorts, doing crosswords.

Next came a stint at the National Theatre. He was Octavius in John Schlesinger's production of *Julius Caesar* with John Gielgud as Caesar, and appeared in 'Michael Bogdanov's romp', *The Hunchback of Notre Dame*. For Ian, the highlight of this production was when he crashed through a brick wall astride a six-foot high wooden horse. But he didn't like the National of those days: 'It was entertainment civil service style.'

His first film was *Jubilee*, in which his co-stars were Adam Ant and Toyah Willcox. Billed as 'the most outrageous motion picture of all time', it was a tale of marauding girl punks, desperate street boys and orgies in Westminster Cathedral. Ian thought the film 'vile and sick-making', but quite amusingly so, and he was pleased at having done it. Derek Jarman, its director, was 'a real artist'.

In 1978 he was back on more familiar ground, playing Shakespeare, this time for the RSC. It was a strong company, including Jonathan Pryce, Jane Lapotaire, Richard Griffiths and Zoë Wanamaker. Ian spent a happy year in Stratford, sharing a flat with his old Edinburgh friend Hilton McRae, playing Tranio in Michael Bogdanov's production of *The Taming of the Shrew* and Ariel in Clifford Williams' *The Tempest*. Bernard Levin in the *Sunday Times* wrote: 'With his Diaghilev mèche and a space voyager's costume, he speaks his lines with a beautiful ghostliness.' And everybody loved his singing as Ariel.

A London season for the RSC followed: a mixture of the unloved *The Innocent* by Tom McGrath in which he played a junkie, jazz playing underground newspaper editor; *Piaf* by Pam Gems which transferred to the West End; and the equally successful movie industry comedy, *Once In a Lifetime*.

It was around this time that Ian's father noticed a newspaper story about the search for a young actor to play the Scottish runner and missionary Eric Liddell in the Hugh Hudson film *Chariots of Fire*. Ian who 'had never run for anything but the bus', had to undergo 'running auditions' before he was given the part. 'I always expected I was going to throw up or collapse,' he said. His preparation for the part included reading the Bible from beginning to end. The Bible, he reported, was 'full of sex and violence'. Liddell's character appealed to him: 'He was a good man. The sort of person we need to have more of,' he said, adding that Liddell showed 'you could win without compromising.'

Before *Chariots of Fire* came out, he made two television Shakespeares, playing Octavius Caesar in *Antony and Cleopatra* and Bertram in *All's Well That Ends Well*. He had also been offered the part of Charlie Andrews, 'another character with Christian zeal', in Richard Attenborough's *Gandhi*. For this film he spent three months filming in India, a country which shocked, moved and attracted him. 'India,' he said 'changed my life.'

Chariots of Fire's success certainly changed his life. It won four Oscars, including the Oscar for best picture of 1981, and became a box-office success. 'It's rare to get the critical acclaim and the money,' said Ian, whose contract had included a percentage of the profits. It made him quite rich. (He was to remain so.) *Chariots* paid for the flat in Beauclerc Road, Hammersmith – opposite a house in which he had been renting a room – where he lived for the remainder of his life. He bought – his one real extravagance – a Mercedes Benz 500 SL drophead. And later he also bought a house for his parents in Edinburgh.

The film had changed him from a highly regarded actor into a celebrity and, potentially, a major movie star. Much of this he relished. He loved being a star at Cannes film festival, meeting Sean Connery and being on friendly terms with Bryan Ferry. He enjoyed being asked to the best dinner parties. Boldly, for a man who had taken part in gay as well as heterosexual relationships but had no intention of telling the world about it, he began making regular sorties to gay clubs. Everywhere he went he was fêted.

But there were aspects of being a celebrity that he strongly resented. He hated the American promotional tour for *Chariots*:

'fifteen interviews a day for three weeks, coast-to-coast'. All they ever asked him about in the chat shows were fame and money. The interviewers couldn't comprehend his jokes. When Ben Cross told a chat show host that to understand his part (a Jewish character) he had consulted a rabbi, Ian added that for his part he had consulted God – and nobody found it funny. Suffering also from unrequited love, Ian eventually abandoned the tour and returned home. 'I don't like being dragged out of my private life into public life,' Ian told an interviewer, adding that he hated being asked for his autograph at parties. 'I enjoy sleeping alone. I'm pretty much of a loner.'

There were self-imposed pressures as well. 'I went through a dodgy patch for about a year afterwards,' he said. 'That kind of success has a strange effect on your personality.'

He agreed to do a succession of American mini-series for 'ridiculous' amounts of money: *The Master of the Game*, promoted as a 'saga of poverty, greed, passion, wealth and corruption'; *Louisiana*, which he found 'a cross between *Dallas* and *Gone With the Wind*', adding, 'I hope it's never shown over here'; and *The Sun Also Rises* – 'never been shown over here, thank God'. He'd sold himself, he thought, and would never do work like that again.

He went on to low-key, but more satisfying work: co-starring with Julie Covington in *Ascendancy*, a film set in Northern Ireland in 1920; taking a small part as a brutal drunk in another Hugh Hudson film, *Greystoke* – a part which appealed to him for cutting across the holy Liddell image: 'I play this wonderful degenerate. The first time you see him he's whipping a little boy.'

In 1982 he was back at the National, this time in much happier circumstances, as Sky Masterson in *Guys and Dolls*, the part played on film by Marlon Brando. He approached rehearsals with gusto. 'I'd been looking for something noisy and cheerful. I like to be happy, dancing, drinking, going wild.' He was rewarded with wonderful reviews. The show was a huge success and his cool, elegant performance widely praised. 'He sings with traces of Sinatra,' wrote the American columnist Rex Reed, 'tap-dances with grace and authority and has a wonderful time throughout.' His singing of 'Luck Be a Lady Tonight' was greeted by audiences as one of the high points of the show.

For *Guys and Dolls* Ian acquired a convincing American accent. In other roles, however, even when not playing a Scot, his Scottish accent was undisguised. 'The Scots tongue is one of the hardest to lose,' he said. And by now Scotland was keen to claim him as one of its finest recent exports. He performed the songs and poetry of Robert Burns, accompanied by the Scottish Chamber Orchestra, and was cast as Bonnie Prince Charlie in Channel 4's *Scotland's Story*. When the *Scottish Daily Record* published an editorial stating 'every nation needs its own heritage of music and drama and its own artists', it listed Ian Charleson as one of those 'who have become internationally renowned to the credit of Scotland'.

Ian returned to the National to play another American part: Eddie in *Fool for Love* by Sam Shepard, a playwright he admired. Several critics noted a new passion and depth in his performance. The play transferred to the West End. Ian was nominated for an Olivier award. And, an added pleasure, his co-star was Julie Walters for whom he had great affection.

A part in Frederic Raphael's TV series *Oxbridge Blues* was a welcome chance to play both comedy and an Englishman. Already, however, by the time it was shown, in November 1984, he was remarking tartly that 'after *Chariots* the scripts didn't exactly flood in,' a theme he was to return to with increasing frequency.

His next foray into comedy was less successful, though it gave him another chance to work with Julie Walters. The script of *Car Trouble* made Ian roar with laughter as he lay in bed reading it, so much so that he found a producer for the film. He played Gerald, 'an absolute prat', who swops his 2CV for an E-type Jaguar with farcical consequences. Sadly, for the film was the last which he completed, *Car Trouble* was panned by the critics and had little success at the box-office.

The year 1986 brought a reunion with his old friends from the RSC, Richard Griffiths and David Lyon, in a production at the Old Vic of *After Aida*, a play about Verdi in which Ian played the librettist Boito.

It was at this time that Ian discovered he was HIV positive. He told very few people. From then on he would react with panic to any marks or rashes on his skin, believing that it could be the first sign of AIDS.

For over a year he turned down all offers of work. 'There's a lot of rubbish around,' he said, and he was waiting for the right job to turn up. He would talk to friends about how frustrated he felt at not having become a movie star. He was resentful at the success of less talented actors. His love-life was, as usual, a source of unhappiness. He blamed himself for never having the long term relationship he craved. He would explain this by saying that he 'always fell in love with the wrong person' – the 'wrong person' being frequently a heterosexual man. He had always had difficulty in accepting his gayness. On one occasion he had told a friend that he hated himself. To another, heterosexual friend, he had said: 'You're a real man. I wish I could be a real man.'

During this period – his first lengthy spell out of work – he spent much of his time pottering around the flat, tending the garden, playing the piano and doing crosswords. 'I can function as a human being without being an actor,' he said afterwards. However, he added: 'I felt a bit sick at heart. I have to be fully occupied both emotionally and mentally, otherwise I'm not very happy. I don't think I'll do it again in a hurry. Memories are very short in this business.'

He returned to work when he was offered a part in a horror film to be made by Dario Argento. Ominously, he was attracted 'as much by the prospect of working in Rome as by the film'. He found the production infuriatingly chaotic. It was no way back to movie stardom. He was involved in a head-on car crash, broke three ribs and split open his knee. Though he was back on the set two days later, he was disturbed by the accident. Afterwards he would refer to it as having particular significance in his life, as being one of the moments when 'things started going wrong'. In a burst of frustration at the filming, he walked off the set before the film was completed and returned home.

He continued to work, however, taking the part of the young major in the television adaptation of J. G. Farrell's novel *Troubles*, and, played another major, this time in the KGB, in the television spy thriller *Codename Kyril*. He enjoyed this part: 'Ever since I was a kid I've wanted to do the things this character does. I get to rush around corners with a gun in my hand.'

Soon afterwards he was back at the National for another American role and another triumph, as Brick in Tennessee Williams' *Cat on a Hot Tin Roof*. He had been hoping for a rest after his television work but 'there are some roles you must do.' It was an emotionally and physically exhausting part, on stage throughout the play, bent double as he hobbled around on a crutch. The production was critically acclaimed, Robert Hewison of *The Times* praising the 'brilliant conviction' of his performance.

It was in the autumn of 1988 that Ian first saw the blotches of karposi sarcoma on his skin and realized that he had AIDS. His reaction over the following weeks was a mixture of panic and an apparent calm. He was losing weight and had developed a cough. Friends calling at his flat would find him still asleep in the early afternoon. That Christmas he went to Edinburgh to see his parents. Shortly after returning to London he was rushed to St Stephen's Hospital in Fulham suffering from pneumonia. For a time he appeared to be close to death. When he had recovered sufficiently, he told his parents the truth about his illness.

In the spring, with his health weakening, he had radiotherapy and then chemotherapy. For some time he had been receiving treatment, including acupuncture, from a holistic doctor.

In June 1989 he returned to the stage to play the role of Greta for a single performance of Martin Sherman's play *Bent* in aid of Stonewall, a group set up to campaign on behalf of the rights of gays and lesbians.

His appearance had begun to attract comment. His face was often badly swollen and his eyes scarcely visible. Though he had told many of his close friends of his condition, the public explanation was that he was recovering from a sinus operation. Rumours that he had AIDS reached the press and several newspapers sent photographers and reporters to his home.

Despite his worsening health he agreed, after much thought, to take over as Hamlet in Richard Eyre's production at the

[xxv]

National. The previous Hamlet, Daniel Day-Lewis had left the cast. Ian felt he was at last emotionally and technically equipped to play the part. He thought and talked endlessly about how he should do it. It was to be the best, the definitive Hamlet.

During rehearsals, members of the cast were struck by his exceptional good humour and sense of fun. He would sometimes break off in the middle of rehearsals to recount amusing stories. His first performance was on 9 October. He had spent the previous two days in the Royal Free Hospital receiving chemo-therapy. As he had expected, audiences were startled by his appearance when he came on stage. Critics mentioned it in their reviews. But they considered his Hamlet to be outstanding. It was, they thought, an original interpretation: Hamlet as a man of reason in an irrational world.

Ill health prevented him from acting at some performances – he was, after all, playing one of the longest parts in Shakespeare. Sometimes he had scarcely enough strength for the final duel. But, though the cast had heard the rumours, the official story remained that he was recovering from a sinus operation. One evening he called a company meeting two hours before they were to go on stage. They knew he wasn't well, he said, and must have been wondering what was wrong. He was enjoying working with them. And he felt they ought to know the truth. He had AIDS and had been suffering from it for some time. When he finished speaking, the members of the company came up to him, one by one, shook his hand or hugged him. One of the older actors said: 'I don't care what you've got. You're the bravest man I know.'

He had played the part for seventeen performances when a review by John Peter appeared in the *Sunday Times*. The review delighted him: 'A masterful new Hamlet', Peter wrote,

'Technically he employs clarity combined with a powerful dramatic drive. His delivery is steely but delicate. The words move with sinuous elegance and crackle with fire. His Hamlet is virile and forceful. He oozes intelligence from every pore.'

'The way Charleson can transform a production', he concluded, 'is a reminder that actors are alive and well, that directors can only draw a performance from those who have one in them and that in the last analysis the voice of drama speaks to us through actors.' This last sentence particularly pleased Ian. Too much importance was generally given to theatre directors and designers, he felt. The review had reaffirmed the importance of the actor.

That Sunday the congratulatory calls poured into Ian's flat. Friends came round with champagne. Ian, while jubilant, was weaker than ever. He had great difficulty in breathing and could scarcely walk across the room. His eyes were thin slits. He had to tilt his head to an abnormal angle in order to see. It seemed impossible to imagine him appearing on stage again.

He was back at the National the following night, 13 November. Several of his friends were in the audience. At the curtain call, most of the audience rose to their feet, clapping and cheering. It was to be his last performance.

The production was due to go to Hong Kong and up to the last moment he was wondering whether to go. He thought he might return to the cast when the production came back to London. His hopes were inexhaustible.

He continued to live at home for most of the last few weeks of his life. A group of friends took it in turns to look after him, cooking, caring for him, fending off callers when Ian was too tired to talk. He continued to look for hope in alternative medicine. He had great difficulty in eating and was very weak.

He died of septicaemia in the early evening of Saturday 6 January 1990.

ALAN BATES

I met Ian when we were both in Simon Gray's *Otherwise Engaged*. It was a particularly happy company. Ian played a surly lodger who took everything for granted and was very bolshy to the landlord. He was marvellous in the part and was immediately accepted by everyone. Though he was the youngest in the cast – still in his early twenties – and it was his first time in the West End, he wasn't overawed. Nor did he play at being the gauche young man. It was simply that, without being arrogant, he was quite fearless and had a natural ease with everybody. There were no barriers for him. My children were very young at the time and when he came to the house he was lovely with them too. I think he was family-conscious in a way which is quite rare in a young man. Once he brought his father and mother to my home. And I remember how proud he was of his sister who had just begun to be a musician.

I also remember when we were on tour, in Oxford, Ian spent a couple of days at the Ashmolean Museum drawing things that appealed to him there. And I realized that he had a rare appreciation of life, an appreciation that went beyond his own job.

Unfortunately I never worked with Ian again, though we were close to one another at other times, meeting through friends. But, without any effort being made on either side, it was a friendship which survived. We had a natural rapport, an ease between us that we could always recapture.

I saw a lot of Ian's work. He brought a tremendous understanding to parts and could convey hidden complexities, not just playing the moment, but playing other moments as well. He was definitely among the top ten actors of his age group. For a long time I thought of him as being lyrical, witty, verging on a character actor, an unusual off-beat romantic. Then, suddenly, in *Fool for Love*, he came up with a physical performance that was full of energy, and extraordinary power. Ian was on his way, really climbing in people's consciousness. It was a career which would have held. He had forty more years' work ahead of him.

I never heard anybody say they didn't like Ian. Not that he made it his business to go around being agreeable to people. But he was loved. He was funny and sharp and could be quite wicked at times. His intelligence allowed him to see people clearly. And he liked them. He also faced life with great honesty. And showed enormous courage towards the end.

A haunting memory I have of Ian is when we were trying to save the site of the Rose Theatre and Ian McKellen had organized a street concert at the site. Ian didn't look well. I think he was already receiving treatment for his illness. But he went onto the concert platform and sang 'My Love is Like a Red, Red Rose'. He could still give himself to a cause like that.

I've heard Ian suddenly burst into song in restaurants. He knew he had a lovely voice and revelled in the pleasure of being able to do something so well. He forgot himself when he sang.

[4]

With elder brother Ken

At school

Aged eighteen

As the herald
in *Marat\Sade*,
DramSoc production
at University, 1969.

The Pantaloonatic, 1970, performed at the Edinburgh Festival
Fringe. *From left to right*: Gordon Roberts, Ian Charleson, David
Rintoul (Wilson), Linda Goddard, Claris Erikson.

Left: With Gavin Reed in *French Without Tears* (1973). *Right*: With Mel Martin in the revival of *Scappino* (1974)

As Claudio in *Much Ado About Nothing* (1974), with Jeremy Irons as Don Pedro and Ian Trigger as Leonato.

Aged twenty-five

In *The Paradise Run* by Howard Brenton for television, 1976.

Ian and Di Trevis paying 50p each to be photographed with 'TV personality', James Aubrey at the Workers' Revolutionary Party's summer fair.

hn Schlesinger's production of *Julius Caesar* at the National in 1977. *From left to ght*: Mark McManus as Mark Anthony, Ian Charleson as Octavius Caesar, Brian Cox as Marcus Brutus.

As Peregrine in Peter Hall's production of *Volpone* at the National (1974) with John Gielgud playing Sir Politic Wouldbe.

Stratford 1977. *From left to right*: Richard Griffiths, Ian, David Lyon, Hilton McRae.

Above: With Hilton McRae.

Right: As Ariel in the RSC production of *The Tempest*, Stratford 1978.

He was taking people somewhere else. For me, his voice always symbolized a special spirit he had. I don't know how you define special spirits: you just know them when you meet them. It was an ability to take himself out of this life.

I think it was thanks to Ian's spirit that he always stayed the same. Success didn't turn him into a spoiled, ridiculous man who believed in his own image. He was wise. He saw life as a whole thing – not as a series of mistakes and accidents. That, I think, must have been the line which gave him an ability to cope with anything, even the appalling illness which killed him.

Shortly before Ian died, I wrote and rang a couple of times saying I would love to see him if he could manage it. I was deeply touched when he said I could come, because I knew he was too ill to see many people. We spoke on the phone before I went round. My hair had been dyed blond when I was filming and I'd kept it that way to make my sons laugh. So I said to Ian: 'Don't get a shock when you see me, because I'm blond.' Ian joked about my blondness and then said, with the same humour: 'Don't get a shock when you see me. It's Quasimodo, baby.' The lightness had stayed with him, thank God. It must have helped him in all he had to undergo.

I saw him two days before he died and found the same lovely character. His spirit had not gone. And our relationship was still there. In spite of all the changes – including the final tragic change – the man I knew had stayed, from his first West End job to our last meeting. When we talked, we discussed mutual friends and he asked after my sons. Eventually he got tired. As he began to fall asleep he was still muttering little jokes.

DAVID PUTTNAM

TEN years ago Hugh Hudson and I had our first meeting over lunch with a young actor named Ian Charleson. The evening before we had been to the theatre to see him starring in *Piaf* and concluded that, after months of searching, we had found our Eric Liddell.

Ian had read the script and lunch was intended to make it easier for the three of us to get to know each other. The conversation was desultory, even a little awkward, especially whenever we got close to the subject of the film.

Months later, with a film and a friendship in the can, I asked him about the strain of that first meeting. 'Didn't you realize how desperate Hugh and I were for you to commit to the film?'

He looked at me incredulously and replied, 'You're joking, I was so scared you wouldn't offer me the part I could hardly speak!' Communication improved thereafter allowing me to enjoy a friendship with an artist I came to admire and adore.

Just before filming, Ian, whose relationship with organized religion was a bit haphazard, asked Colin Welland if he would mind if he selected and paraphrased the sections of the Bible he was required to preach from. 'How well do you know the Bible?' asked Colin.

'I've almost finished it,' was the reply. And he had – the most closely annotated copy I've ever seen became the basis for a series of scenes played with such conviction that Eric Liddell's widow, when she saw the finished film, made this judgement: 'You know, Eric's great sadness was that he was a poor preacher – he had bags of conviction but lacked a way with words. Your Mr Charleson made it all come right. He said what Eric always wanted to say, and to millions of people all around the world. That would have made Eric very happy.'

In the autumn of 1989 Hugh Hudson and I were once again sitting in a restaurant with Ian. Again the conversation had become stilted, but this time we were saved from awkwardness by Ian looking straight at us and saying, 'I have AIDS you know.' Hugh handled the moment well, whilst I gazed glassy-eyed at the table-cloth and mumbled something incoherent and, I hope, incomprehensible. Ian wouldn't allow our conversation to take refuge in the past: that would have been too easy.

Indeed, far more than us, he was very much in the here and now, preparing for the National Theatre's production of *Hamlet* and the tour of Japan that promised to follow.

It was important to him that he fought his grotesque illness with everything he had and, if he couldn't beat it, then he was desperately keen at least to strike a blow against it. From that point on, Ian won every battle except the very last. His Hamlet was a triumph and the dignity with which he faced dying was beyond belief.

The decision, with the equally courageous agreement of his family, not to equivocate about the cause of his death, may well have been an important small step in preventing ill-considered and reactionary opinion from stifling the urgency of the debate, upon which rests any possibility for the prevention and eventual cure of AIDS.

HILTON McRAE

How do you dissect a friendship?

It began at university in Edinburgh. Both of us upper-working-class lads wanting to be actors. Ian from Edinburgh, living at home, and me from Dundee. Ian, a year above me, studying for an arts degree. Already a star of DramSoc, a golden boy, the best dancer I'd ever met, flamboyant, a great mover on stage. When Ian played the herald in a DramSoc production of *Marat/Sade*, no one in the audience could keep their eyes off him.

A promising actor already. But also funny, charming and delicious to be with. And so we became friends, would go to parties together – where everyone tried to copy Ian's dancing – played bridge or stayed up till four in the morning talking, not about Stanislavsky or Peter Brook, but about our parents, being Scottish, clothes, music, the best bidding system at bridge and painting. (Ian, who'd started by doing a degree in architecture, went to lectures in Fine Art even though they weren't part of his course, just because he thought the lecturer was brilliant.) In all these things – apart from bridge – Ian either knew most or was the most receptive to new ideas, and he would wrap it all up and lay it out as a Universal Principle. It wasn't that he was more educated or more intelligent than the rest of us. But somehow when I talked with him, I felt closer to understanding things than I ever had before.

Revolution seemed as though it wasn't far off – this was the late sixties – and we were sure the world was a good sort of place and that we had most of the answers. We also knew we were going to be actors. It seemed easy at the time. Nobody ever contemplated the possibility of being out of work or anything like that. One of our best friends, David Rintoul, had got a place at RADA, so it seemed quite natural when Ian finished his degree and was accepted by LAMDA.

Off he went to London to become an actor, eventually found a flat in St John's Wood and, since he didn't have a grant, was exceptionally hard up. For a time he worked in the evenings, singing in a restaurant, and people helped him out. One day Alec Guinness sent him a caseful of clothes and a cheque. I suppose people were helpful because they recognized he had a special talent. But his extraordinary charm must have smoothed the way as well.

Then I came down to London, moved into his flat and found him a part-time job at the Hard Rock Café in Park Lane where I worked. The waitresses adored him. We were 'bus-boys', which meant we cleared the tables: the dancing bus-boys, in actual fact, because they played such loud music that we danced all over the place. The Hard Rock had just opened, the first authentic American hamburger joint in London, and was full of glamorous people, or so it seemed. Mind you, nobody was as glamorous as us.

Ian didn't stay long at the Hard Rock. Soon he was with the Young Vic, playing Jimmy Porter in *Look Back in Anger* and

Hamlet in *Rosencrantz and Guildenstern Are Dead*, while I
went on to do political theatre (and used to be quite scathing
about how he'd gone into the established theatre instead of the
real, committed stuff).

He could easily have been big-headed, getting a great acting
job almost straight from drama school. But he wasn't. Ian was
never big-headed, even after *Chariots of Fire* was such a big
success. A kind of Scottish puritan quality always saved him
from that.

And so our lives kept on crossing and intertwining. Quite
often we shared flats and for a year we worked together for the
RSC in Stratford. When I think about my friendship with Ian, it
seems that Stratford was probably the very best time we had
together (and we had lots of great times). We would be twenty-
eight or twenty-nine. Ian was Tranio in *The Taming of the
Shrew* and Ariel in *The Tempest*. The reviews were good, sometimes good enough to make him whoop with joy. Our home
was a converted stables six miles out of town in lovely countryside with a private tennis court. (Ian played tennis with unerring
ineptitude.) We also played cards and board games, talked to
friends, drank, sang, played piano duets – we did a lot of playing
of one sort or another – and just lounged about. And Ian was
very happy, I think. The only black spot was the rehearsals for
The Tempest. He hated them. As a gesture of discontent, Ian
wore a long green overcoat throughout and never took his hands
out of his pockets. 'Ariel?' said Richard Griffiths, who was in
the same production. 'He's definitely VHF – a Very Heavy Fairy.'

But it wasn't for Ian's heaviness that most people remember
that production of *The Tempest*, it was for his singing. The
RSC even brought out a record of his songs. Ian's singing was
extraordinary: a high tenor voice with an ethereal quality that

[17]

is impossible to describe. When he sang, time stopped. Later, much later, fourteen months before he died, at David Rintoul's fortieth birthday party at L'Escargot, Ian sang 'My Love is Like a Red, Red Rose' and sang it so beautifully that most of us cried and a waiter brought him a rose.

Ian was much liked in Stratford. But then he was much liked everywhere he went. Actors loved working with him. His vulnerability and openness meant that people always knew where he stood. Perhaps his greatest quality on stage was his sensitivity to the other actors. And everyone was attracted by his looks, his wit, his grace. His story-telling was hilarious (a table-full of listeners would end up helpless with laughter), sharp with his observations. And, as in Edinburgh, his talk often moved towards trying to understand some truth about life or the universe. There was often an edge to his humour, a mocking, sardonic streak. In restaurants, actors who were table-hopping could end up victims of his wit – and yet Ian would do even this so engagingly that they felt nothing but pleasure.

As I've said, Ian wasn't big-headed. But, I have to add, he wasn't unduly modest either. Once he told me how, as a boy, he would look out of his bedroom window and see the gorse growing on the slopes of Arthur's Seat. He noticed how the gorse appeared to form the shape of the initials I.C. 'And that, Hilty', he said, 'was when I knew I was destined to be a great actor.' And he wanted to be not just great, but the very greatest.

But there was another strand to his character: a vein of self-mockery alongside the ambition and self-confidence. That came out in many of his favourite stories. Such as the time we were coming out of the stage door at Stratford, and two American girls stopped him, asking for his autograph. Ian had just done another stint as Ariel, a part for which, in some scenes, he wore an enormous white ruff. When he'd given the autographs, one of the girls paused, clearly with something on her mind. Finally she said: 'Do you mind if I ask you something?'

'Sure,' said Ian.

'Well,' she said, 'when you come on with that thing round your neck, is that to show you've turned into a sea-nymph?'

'Yes. That's exactly right,' said Ian, pleased that someone had understood the rather obscure reasoning behind his costume.

'Mmmm,' said the girl, 'you didn't make it.'

He was a good friend, perhaps the best I'll ever have. Open, loving, generous in spirit.

Yes, he was my best friend. Most days if we weren't to meet, we would talk to one another on the phone. And we always knew what the other was thinking. I saw things through his eyes as well as my own. I thought I knew all about him.

But it wasn't until he was dying that I realized what courage he had. That was courage playing Hamlet when he was so weak and could hardly breathe. His face puffed up. Eyes almost lost in his face. Scarcely recognizable. And yet he could joke about even that. 'When I walk on stage', he told me before the first night, 'all you'll hear is people turning the pages of their programmes and saying, "Who's that? Who's that?"'

That part meant so much to him. He wanted to play all the great roles – and be great in them. 'This disease is a real bastard,' he said. 'I want to go on and do my Benedick and my Richard II and then one day do my King Lear.' His understanding of theatrical technique at its peak, he knew exactly what he wanted to do. Only his body could let him down.

Ian told me how, if he had to die, he would like it to be. On the stage of the National Theatre, with the words 'the rest is

[19]

silence'. Though his powers were magical and his timing normally perfect, even he couldn't manage that final gesture. But
the desire was typical of the man. Flamboyant, witty, brave.

DI TREVIS

WHEN I first knew Ian Charleson in the early seventies he was rather spotty and invariably late. We were sharing with other young actors a bleak flat in Belgrave Gardens on the borders of Kilburn. Antony Sher lived up the road. My earliest memory is of sitting on the edge of the bath talking to Ian as he peered into the bathroom mirror scrubbing medical cleanser into his face and cursing. He had just left LAMDA early, with some relief, to start his first job at the Young Vic. He'd had to pay his way through drama school by working at night serving hamburgers in the Hard Rock Café. His fellow students, sad that he could not pay his fees one term, had collected money together to help him, pretending it came from an anonymous well-wisher. Someone had told Alec Guinness of a penniless and talented student and Guinness had sent him money, a charming letter and some clothes. Ian wore one of the shirts – silk with a dull mauve stripe – for years. He was still wearing it in his first season at Stratford when both elbows showed through the sleeves. He liked his old clothes. He wore his favourite ones all the years I knew him: long green mackintosh, tan leather boots, button-up jeans and an old brown belt.

[23]

At the Young Vic, Frank Dunlop's company got so fed up with waiting for Ian that they clubbed together to buy him a radio alarm clock for his birthday that August. He must have been twenty-two or three. The alarm clock made no difference. It was not just that he could sleep longer and deeper than anyone I knew, he seemed congenitally incapable of punctuality. But, with a smile and a word, he got away with it. I always had the feeling that from childhood onwards he'd been easy to forgive like a fallen angel in an Italian painting. I've seen him roll up so late for dinner we were all eating pudding. You'd be furious as he entered the room and then somehow it evaporated. You were glad to see Ian.

He'd had luck as a young actor. Getting work never seemed to be a problem. But then from the beginning he was brimming with talent and talent somehow makes its own luck. There seemed nothing he couldn't do. Slim, graceful and intelligent, he could act, sing and dance. He'd been good in *Look Back in Anger* and soon he went off to play Hamlet. Directors sometimes said he was 'too Scottish'. This infuriated him. Once someone told him his face was so pock-marked he'd never work on film. It's hard to credit the casual cruelties a young actor suffers.

How did we pass our time in those days? We worked hard if only we could. We smoked the obligatory dope, listened to records, played games. We talked about plays, about the theatre. We tried not to mention ambition because we were all so ambitious and just under the surface, especially in the presence of this golden boy, lurked envy. People loved Ian but they envied him, and no wonder. At parties I could always get a laugh by listing his attributes: blond hair; good looks; marvellous actor; sings like a dream; speaks French; plays piano; paints; draws

[24]

and wins at Monopoly. 'For all our sakes', I'd add, 'let's hope he's unhappy at home.'

Ian always loved playing games – Monopoly, backgammon, Diplomacy, mah jong. He had a long craze for enormous, complicated jigsaws. He would spend hours pouring patiently over pieces of sky with my then twelve-year-old sister, Sarah, or sit with her long into the night over a game of mah jong, the ivory tiles clicking in the lamplight. Peering at a bad hand he would mutter 'Fuck-my-old-boots-don't-repeat-that-Sarah' all in one breath. There were times we only cursed in cod French – 'pierre les corbeaux' – and had competitions as to who could think up the silliest exclamations. Ian invariably won. Later, when we shared a flat in Gloucester Crescent, we'd get up early to play a game of mah jong before rehearsals. Ian, by that time, was rehearsing Octavius in *Julius Caesar* at the National Theatre. He was always late for those rehearsals too. I never saw him walk out of the door, he always ran. He reckoned it would take fifteen minutes on a bike from Camden Town to the South Bank, but it never did. He would bicycle up to Soho at the end of rehearsals, have a swim, eat something healthy at Cranks ('for my skin') before he tore back for the evening performance, late no doubt for the half. He was always full of new enthusiasms – a book, a diet, a record. By then, he'd been in his first West End success, *Otherwise Engaged*, and when it was in Oxford on tour we spent a few hilarious days together at the Turf Tavern where Ian and I, by that time with a craze for yoga, tried to teach Nigel Hawthorne to stand on his head.

He played the young student in *Otherwise Engaged*. I remember the moment during the first night when I sat in the circle of the Queen's Theatre and suddenly realized what Ian's secret was. He showed no anxiety to please. The audience could take

[25]

him or leave him. He didn't seem to care. This gave his acting its precision and economy. He seemed to do nothing. All his work was aimed at effortlessness. In acting, he loathed excess, physical or emotional. When in the last year some tantalizing reserve broke deep down in him, his work became riveting. Oddly enough, I can hardly remember the performances save the last *Hamlet* and a workshop *Measure for Measure* – at Peter Gill's Riverside Studios. As Angelo Ian was able to portray such tortured complexity of desire and self-reproach that it surely sprang from an ambivalence of his own.

It is his off-stage self that remains vivid. One of his great loves was travel. He might be late but he didn't miss planes. If you wanted a travelling companion the first person you thought of was Ian. Quite simply, he was fun. We once travelled through the Greek islands for six weeks, each carrying one shoulder bag containing T-shirts, swimming things, toilet bag and a book – his was *The Brothers Karamazov*. To deal with strangers we met on our way, he invented a code. According to the tune we hummed, it went: 'I like this person. Let's stay' or 'I loathe this person. Let's go.' More rarely: 'I really like this person. You go.'

I don't want to give the impression that he was relentlessly entertaining for he could spend hours in companionable silence; and in conversation about politics or work was uncompromisingly tough. On the other hand, it has to be said, he was hilarious: lightning flashes of mimicry, the wry throwaway line, the perfectly placed anecdote. It was he who after a hot afternoon on dusty Cretan streets coined the phrase 'hard-hearted Chania'. Once we were dropped at a deserted crossroads by a country bus and after walking for hours we hitched a lift on the open back of a lorry to within sight of the sea at Plakias. Ian with a cry of joy broke into his Ethel Merman imitation: 'They say that falling in love is wonderful. It's wonderful, so they say.' And the W-O-N-D-E-R-F-U-L echoed through those Aegean hills.

That summer he sang a lot. 'La Vie en Rose' (how well he spoke French) and every morning 'The Sun Has Got His Hat On'. One day we took a boat to an empty bay to learn to water ski and as we sailed through a turquoise sea, he sang old Scottish ballads, 'The Twa Corbies', 'Among the Blooming Heather' and 'My Love is Like a Red, Red Rose'. He had a voice like a silver stream. In the pitch black darkness of a Greek Easter night we walked up a hillside, our only light candles which splashed hot wax on our hands (lots of muttered 'Fuck-my-old-boots') to hear, in one of the mountain villages, the priest call out at midnight 'Kyrie Eleison' and the crowd burst into song.

Ian loved music: of his record collection I remember lots of Brahms – especially the violin concerto in an old recording by a virtuosic Belgian violinist whose name eludes me – and a very slow fifties version of the Pachelbel canon. He also loved, as he put it, 'black women screaming' – Tina Turner, Aretha Franklin and a marvellous version of that song half-spoken, half-sung, where, as the bride approaches the altar at a wedding, a girl cries out 'It Should Have Been Me' – his theme song, as he used to remark bitterly. Ironically, he knew well the pangs of disprized love. He once poignantly described the miasma of unresolved feeling and heartbreak that hung over his university days. Even at the height of his success, during an American promotional tour of *Chariots of Fire*, he missed someone so bitterly he flew home, knowing, he told me, 'full well' that his absence had hardly been noticed and his love would remain unspoken.

We were in Crete when on 1 May Saigon was liberated and at dinner we toasted the victory. Later we fell into conversation

[27]

with an American who said he had worked in Vietnam for the CIA. His speciality was discovering, from studying the outside, what a parcel held on the inside. 'Don't look at me,' Ian said, 'You'll never guess.'

And I don't suppose many of us ever did quite. Despite his charm and warmth, at his innermost core lay a certain diffidence, a spiritual untouchability. It was not that he could not talk of his feelings. He did, articulately. Nor do I think that he was more reserved with women. But, *au fond*, he was a solitary person. He had what amounted to a horror almost of the dependency that imtimacy brings. Perhaps this is why he had such a talent for friendship, picking up the threads easily after long absences but by the same token leaving again on a word and a wave, without heartache. Perhaps this also accounts for his lateness – those five, ten, fifteen minutes rehearsed again his dread of being needed, of being necessary.

When he raised his glass to the end of the Vietnam War it was no idle gesture. Ian was a socialist and with success and wealth, his views never changed. He never forgot his origins in the Scottish working class. He was proud of his people: canny, thrifty, succinct. He hated hyperbole. Once in a dressing-room someone was describing the actor Richard Griffiths, whom Ian sincerely admired, as 'brilliant, brilliant – in fact an absolute genius'. 'What do you mean?' asked Ian incredulously, 'like Beethoven?'

When, after *Chariots of Fire*, he did buy a flat of his own, his tastes stayed simple and unostentatious – a piano, comfortable sofas, a log fire and a bedroom looking out over the green of a small garden. The car he chose though was uncharacteristically glamorous: a blue Mercedes convertible. He loved it as one loves a childhood dream come true. It belonged on sunny roads speeding south. And he did look like a dream of success in it with his blond hair and dark glasses. In London, though, he'd still ride to the theatre on his bike. A friend, seeing him cycling past her on the street outside the National Theatre in a mohair sweater, his heavy bicycle lock and chain swinging around his neck, thought he looked 'the most beautiful man in the world'. Then he stopped and chatted and she realized it was 'just Ian'.

As is so often the case, he had more problems in the years after success than before. Somehow a big film career didn't materialize. He turned down a lot of work in England hoping, I suspect, for the film offer that didn't come. 'What's Ian doing?' I would ask. 'Nothing', would come the answer. He was restless. He could be bitter. He'd talk with more animation of the rubbish he'd turned down than enthusiasm for any new project. Although we met rarely in the late eighties we would sometimes bump into each other backstage and have lunch together. He'd still fish an old tobacco tin out of his jeans pocket and roll up a minute cigarette that he hardly smoked. (When he'd made *Gandhi* in India I was sent an urgent message: SEND TINS OLD HOLBORN.) We'd talk. I'd laugh. He'd go. He seemed alone, surrounded by friends.

On an impulse late one night in 1989, I telephoned him. We hadn't spoken for months but I'd heard that our mutual friend Philip Sayer was ill with lung cancer and had rung thinking Ian would know how best I could help. How ironic my opening remarks must have seemed! Ian told me he had AIDS. Although in February a doctor had given him a year to live, he was hopeful, keen to fight, full of plans – 'I just don't feel as if I'm dying.'

Despite his fears ('A year's not long, you know') and the sadness of his family, he was happier at moments than he'd ever been. Life took on a piercing clarity. One of the happinesses of his last year was that he realized the simple kindness of ordinary people. When he'd been crying one morning in his hospital room and tried, unsuccessfully, to eat lunch ('Well, actually Di, one grape') an elderly lady, a retired beautician had come in and offered to manicure his nails. Small and grey-haired, she had come to the AIDS ward as a volunteer because years before her young husband, dying of TB, had been shunned 'as if he had plague'. As Ian wept, she took his hands in hers and talked. 'She was just an ordinary wee woman, but in her way a kind of saint.'

He had feared a flu or pneumonia but could never have imagined the particularly cruel route his illness would take. His sinuses filled. His eyes became swollen, then his forehead and jowls. All his youthful anxieties about his face returned tenfold. He evolved a theory that the virus attacked at the psychologically most vulnerable point. He knew a dancer, for instance, whose legs were afflicted. AIDS was subtle. It tried to destroy you spiritually first. The rest was then easy. He personalized the virus to fight it, as if it resembled some punishing Edinburgh schoolmaster. The only way for him to fight back was to give up any inhibition about his appearance. 'But I'm beginning to look altogether prettier', he quipped, 'like Felicity Kendal with a beard.' He put on dark glasses and faced the world. And went back to the National Theatre to play Hamlet.

During the weeks of those rehearsals he fought bitterly as symptoms worsened and new problems arose. One Saturday he rehearsed the sword fight and then drove up to the Royal Free Hospital in Hampstead where he had to get into bed for the overnight drip of chemotherapy. By Sunday evening, he was still suffering side effects and the doctor forbade him to leave. He persuaded a nurse to bring him his clothes, promising he'd simply get dressed and wait for the doctor. She caught him as

[30]

he was leaving the ward. 'You promised,' she said. 'At this point', Ian said, 'I don't keep promises.'

His sole objective was to get to rehearsals in the morning looking as if he'd spent the weekend relaxing in front of the television. Later chemotherapy gave way to radiotherapy which required him to lie with lead coverings over his eyeballs, and gave him a vile combination of claustrophobia and nausea. If he took drugs to reduce the swelling, vomiting made him unable to work. If he took antibiotics he suffered enormous mouth ulcers, making it impossible to eat or speak. Another drug would be prescribed to chase the ill effects of the previous one and would, in time, cause side effects of its own. But everything now was subservient to *Hamlet*: to rehearse the play; to appear to be recovering from his sinus operation; to support, not drain the rest of the cast. No one remotely guessed how ill Ian really was or how much his famed effortlessness was costing him in sweat and tears. As Michael Bryant, who played Polonius said later, 'He was a brave gentleman.'

The golden boy had come of age.

When he came on stage as Hamlet I was plunged into a kind of panic when, for a moment, I didn't recognize him at all: he had the face of a complete stranger. In other ways too there were changes. His voice had a new and vibrant depth, probably because he could no longer rely on his head voice and reached deep down for the breath and resonance. Emotionally, he was so free there was absolutely no censure, no gap between impulse and utterance. The words, the complexity of thought and expression had become, at the profoundest level, his. In the last scene, came a feeling which was incalculably terrible. As 'Hamlet' lay dying, his face obscured for a moment in Horatio's arms, his doublet rode up and with a jolt of recognition I suddenly saw the old Ian – the long curve of his waist, the fall of his hair. I remembered a flash of light on water and Ian skiing across a blue bay. My throat scorched with anguish.

Later as he dragged on an old T-shirt and jeans, drinking and laughing in his dressing-room, my sister told him of her forthcoming marriage and he asked to be sent an invitation. 'It's in February,' she added, unknowingly. There was a short silence.

'I'd love to come', he smiled, 'if I'm not . . .' a pause as he put on his dark glasses, 'busy.' If it was a performance it seemed, as always, effortless.

He died weeks short of the year he'd been given, on 6 January 1990. This time he was not late, but, for those of us who loved him, much much too early.

HUGH HUDSON

Run the Straight Race

LONDON 1989

In death, as in life, Ian Charleson was honest and true, and very brave. He faced dying with a princely nobility that was an inspiration to all who knew and loved him. I saw him quite often during those final months as he raced time, battling this awful condition. He thought somehow he would beat it – that he was the one who could. Bodily, of course, he was like all of us – frail and vulnerable. It was his spirit that was special – inextinguishable.

WEST AFRICA 1984

Greystoke, the Legend of Tarzan Lord of the Apes was a near faithful telling of the Tarzan legend as written by Edgar Rice Burroughs in the first book. This twentieth-century mythic tale deals with man's primate instincts, the question of nurture versus nature and ends with the brutal realization that life in civilized society can often be more barbaric than life in the tropical rain forest. *Greystoke* starred Sir Ralph Richardson and Ian Holm and introduced Andie McDowell and Christophe Lambert to the screen. It was filmed in the West African republic of Cameroon and at Elstree Studios.

Ian accepted a small role in the film. During the eighteen-month production period his mischievous, charming company brought laughter and joy to lighten the most arduous of experiences. Unfailingly Ian would spot the ironies of any situation, and his ability to seek-out the essential truth in people, though a shock to many, was a gift it would have been foolish to deny or reject.

Ian became a firm friend to the young and almost inexperienced French actor, Christophe Lambert, who had been chosen for the lead in the film. Ian gave Christophe unconditional personal and artistic support, bolstering him up and coaching him to become the fine romantic lead he was. He never showed an iota of envy or competition, as many young actors in his position might have done, and Christophe could not have handled the role without Ian's encouragement.

EDINBURGH 1980

Chariots of Fire is a film that has had a charmed life. I believe, however, its true achievement is in the almost perfect casting of the characters, not only the three central roles but every supporting character. Ben Cross as the neurotic, relentless, ambitious Abrahams, driven to succeed and 'show' the world. Nigel Havers perfectly embodied the self-confident, aristocratic and forever charming Lord Lindsay, his conciliatory nature ideally able to deal with both the Prince of Wales, the Olympic Committee and Eric Liddell's uncompromising stand not to run on Sunday. And, of course, Ian Charleson who completely and instinctively understood Liddell's motivations. The same applied to John Gielgud, Lindsay Anderson, Nigel Davenport, Ian Holm, Richard Griffiths, Nicholas Farrell, Cheryl Campbell and Alice Krige.

[36]

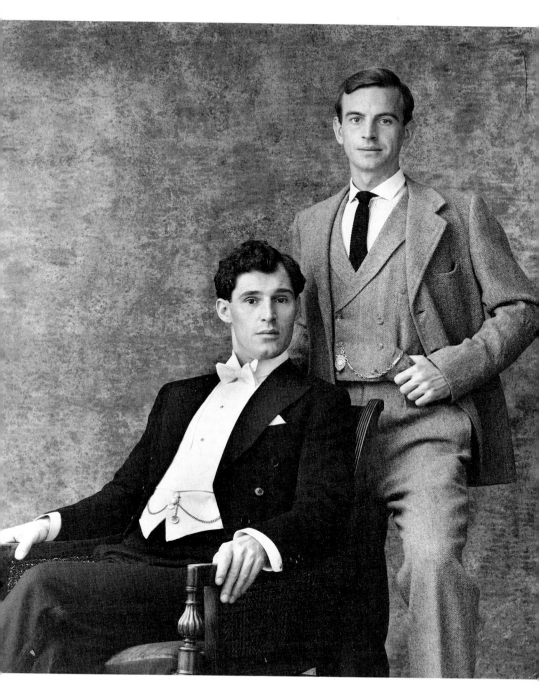

Photographed by Snowdon for *Chariots of Fire* with Ben Cross, 1981.

As Eric Liddell, racing against Harold Abrahams for the first time.

With Cheryl Campbell.

Nigel Havers, Ian and Ben Cross at the Cannes Film Festival.

As Eric Liddell, the Scottish missionary.

Celebrating success at Cannes. The stars of *Chariots* (*from left to right*), Nigel Havers
Ian, Hugh Hudson, Ben Cross, Colin Welland and David Puttnam.

The Olympic team returning (from *Chariots of Fire*).

With Ben Kingsley in *Gandi*, 1982.

Touring the British Film Year Roadshow.

In rehearsal for Richard Eyre's production of *Guys and Dolls* at the National Theatre, 1982.

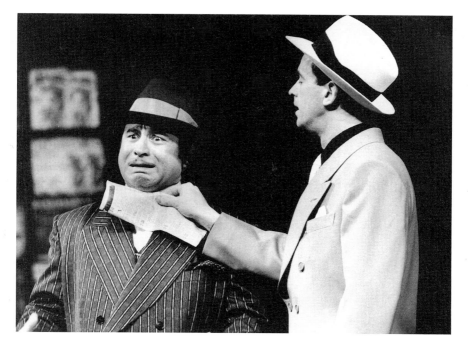

As Sky Masterson, with Bob Hoskins as Nathan Detroit.

Overleaf: Photographed by Johnny Rozsa in Los Angeles, 1983.

We arrived early at the rugby ground to film perhaps the most important scene for the Eric Liddell character. The scene centred around an evangelical address to a working men's rugby football crowd. Two days earlier Ian had come to me, together with Cheryl Campbell who played his sister in the film. He felt unable to deal with the words as scripted, which he thought sanctimonious and portentous. It was decided that *he* should pen words which he *could* speak.

That morning he was still unprepared. One hour before filming began we were sitting in the car structuring the scene using passages from the Bible chosen by Ian and long pieces that he had written. The scene was to be filmed in one continuous take to keep the authenticity that too many cut away shots would have destroyed. Naturally, Ian could never have remembered the new words in time, and he had the inspired idea of hiding the text inside the crown of his hat. As Liddell starts the address, off comes the hat. Look at the scene and you will see Ian glancing down in a gesture which, for the unaware, seems quite natural as Liddell searches (literally) for the words with which to express his feelings.

Ian was embarking on a career which would show him to be pre-eminent among the actors of his generation. He cast a spell on the whole enterprise of *Chariots*, projecting a 'light' onto the film that seemed to shine through the character of Liddell into the whole company. Movingly written by Colin Welland, the film was brought to life by Ian in a way that Colin could never have even hoped for. It was the most joyous eleven weeks of filming.

Such was the bond, and the pleasure of working with Ian; a sense of feeling 'at home' with him, that whenever I embarked on a new film, I always would ask myself – where is the role for Ian?

[37]

Ian Charleson and Eric Liddell were strangely similar. Both came from Edinburgh, both had lives cut short in their primes and both were never afraid to speak the truth – a rare quality.

A modesty inhabited Ian's art. He gave truth to his work and a real generosity to his colleagues – unlike most of us, he was rarely threatened by the success of others and clearly saw through the mendacity and mediocrity that is so prevalent in the world where he chose to express his talents.

As an artist he possessed the sense of timing that makes great singers, musicians, composers and, of course, great actors: that knife-edge moment of pause and tension so essential to performance – be it comedy or tragedy, musical or romance. Ian was able to master them all.

And those words, from *Chariots of Fire*, that he wrote himself seem perfectly to sum up all he was about:

You came to see a race today, to see someone win – happened to be me. But I want you to do more than just watch a race. I want you to take part in it. I want to compare faith to running in a race. It's hard – requires concentration of will, energy of soul. You experience elation, when the winner breaks the tape – specially if you've got a bet on it. But how long does that last? You go home – maybe your dinner is burnt, maybe you haven't got a job. So who am I to say – believe – have faith in the face of life's realities. I would like to give you something more permanent, but I can only point the way. I have no formula for winning the race. Everyone runs in their own way, or in his own way. Then where does the power come from to see the race to its end? From within. Jesus said, 'Behold the kingdom of God is with you, if with

[38]

all your hearts you truly seek me ye shall ever surely find me.'
If you commit yourself to the love of Christ, then *that* is how
you run a straight race.

Ian's uncompromising life force gave him a direction and an
unswerving sense of right and wrong. His ability to combine
lightness of touch with depth of truth; his mischievous sense of
humour, which always prevented events and situations from
becoming too serious or ponderous; his unfailing loyalty that
begat loyalty – all added such richness to life that without him
it will be so much poorer.

ELIZABETH CHARLESON

THROUGHOUT my childhood and teenage years, Ian was my ally and protector, the instigator of my love of the arts and of my own artistic beginnings.

I have vivid memories of him in the early days on stage in the university theatrical productions, and loved to go along to rehearsals, relishing every role he played. It seemed to me at the time that I was the only girl in the world who had such an extraordinary brother. I was so enthralled when he played Malvolio in *Twelfth Night* that I learned his soliloquys and recited them to my unfortunate class of fellow eight-year-olds. Ian was always happy to have me tag along, despite the ten-year age difference, and I was very excited when he gave me a non-speaking child-role in one of the student productions. My father and the university chaplain, who were not in the swing of the progressive sixties, were horrified to discover me proudly on stage in a play in which all the adult female roles were topless.

My musical appreciation began with *Peter and the Wolf*. Ian would put the record on and act all the parts out. I was always reduced to a screaming wreck whenever 'wolf' appeared. I listened to all his records and, by the time I was twelve, I was familiar with many composers, though I did have problems digesting Stravinsky's *Rite of Spring*. Whatever Ian played on the piano, I wanted to learn too, and we often played simple duets together.

When he finally went to London, Ian left behind beautiful books on art and some great masterpieces of literature. And because they belonged to him, I made special efforts to read them. His love of the arts rubbed off onto me, and the steps I took which eventually led me into life as a professional musician were shaped and encouraged by Ian. Many years later we were, by coincidence, working in the same town. Next day in the local paper there were articles about each of us, and, looking at our photographs side by side, it gave me quite a thrill to think that he might be proud of me, too.

When I went to London to study, where Ian had for many years been pursuing a blossoming career, we had to get to know each other all over again. It's strange how the habits of a lifetime die hard, because, despite the fact that we shared a lot over the years, I suppose I was always considered to be the baby of the family, and Ian never really gave up his role of protector. Once, when I had flu, he came rushing over with bottles of vitamin C, garlic capsules, yoghurt, bags of fruit and flowers and wouldn't leave until I had had large doses of everything.

Protecting his family and the people he loved was an inherent part of Ian's nature. His advice, when required, was always offered on the basis of him having listened honestly and patiently. He shared a great deal of his life with his family and took delight in including us in his latest project. We went to every play he was ever in and somehow Ian always contrived to get us into private film previews, or on set watching the filming and rehearsing. He wasn't content just to have us there – he liked to introduce us to his fellow actors and crew. I think the only time he was surprised to see me was when I turned up unexpectedly at his apartment at two a.m. in a remote part of Louisiana where he was making a mini-series. Though he was surprised, he was delighted to see me.

Ian loved to see us enjoying ourselves. He brought much excitement and wonderful discoveries to our lives, broadening our minds and challenging our ideas and complacencies. In fact Ian was a great observer and challenger of life, and behind his observations there existed a wry sense of humour which often highlighted all our follies and tragedies. On frequent occasions he would have us rolling around laughing at ourselves. Even though he was very poorly last Xmas, he wanted to enjoy the festivities with family and friends. I have memories of a lovely evening with Ian in a tartan blanket on a friend's couch, regailing us with hilarious stories about one of his student summers working in a pea-canning factory. It was a special night.

I think I admired Ian for his belief in himself and the courage he had to look for the truth in all situations. The last year of his life encapsulated the essence of Ian. His bravery, humour and unfailing honesty were there throughout in the face of impending death.

DAVID RINTOUL

I AN's funeral was on a typical Edinburgh day, blustery with a patchy grey-blue sky. About thirty or forty of us came, old friends and relatives, as many people as could fit into his parents' front room. There was a great deal of grief. A minister, from the church his parents attend, spoke to us. The cemetery was in Portobello, near to where Ian was brought up, overlooking the sea. I remember the pile of earth on a tarpaulin beside the open grave. The Edinburgh day, the grave in Portobello, the view of the sea — there seemed a sort of rightness to it, ghastly as it was.

When Ian died one of my fears was that I would remember him only as he was towards the end, for I spent a lot of time with him in the last few months when he was physically weak and sick. But that has not happened. Though it's hard to get it into proportion, the illness was only a short part of his life.

Just as water is a good conductor of electricity, Ian was a good conductor of something: you might call it life-force or optimism. A lightness of being. He could create it or receive it from other people and pass it on. Once when we went on holiday together to Greece, I felt most strongly a power he had, the power to tap into an idyll. It seemed the same when I visited Ian and our friend Hilton when they were living near Stratford. An idyll.

Ian acted the way he was. Ian as an actor was a natural with enormous charm. Walking on stage he would command the house in an effortless way, making the audience feel that everything was all right, that they were in safe hands. He had a quality that was attractive and watchable, and an ease that was immediately appealing.

So many people rang up wanting to talk to him when he was very ill. Sometimes when I answered the phone I would have to tell them that Ian was too weak or tired to talk to them – and I realized how hurt they were. And I understood what a good friend Ian was to a lot of people. He was important to them. He played a large part in their lives.

I was his friend for twenty-two years. The essential Ian never seemed to change.

I'd been at Edinburgh University for a year when he arrived, newly eighteen and straight from school. From the start I felt he was a kindred spirit, the first person I'd met who really confirmed the way I felt about things. Like me, Ian came from the east coast of Scotland, which can be a dour, depressing and repressive place. He'd been through all that and come out full of optimism and energy. We egged each other on. And he shared my obsession with the theatre.

Absolutely an obsession. We were in love with the theatre. In three years at university I acted in thirty plays, directing some more, and Ian must have done as much. We were the young turks in DramSoc, part of a huge release of energy. It was a great time to be in Edinburgh and not just as regards university plays: the Traverse was burgeoning, Richard Eyre was at the Lyceum. We were lucky to be involved.

We were lucky also, I think, that the university didn't have a drama department (where the lecturers would have directed the plays). We did it all ourselves and took on a lot of commitment and responsibility. The two years we had at Edinburgh together gave us a mutual understanding and a sense of something shared that lasted throughout our friendship.

Our first production together was *Twelfth Night*. I was a truly dreadful Sir Toby Belch, drunk every night on stage because that seemed right for the part, and Ian was a wonderful Malvolio. People recognized his talent right away.

Ian, who was a good painter as well, designed costumes for some of our shows, arousing the wrath of a local councillor when, following Ian's designs, two actresses appeared bare-breasted on stage in a production of *The Flies*.

There was a great bond between us. We were almost insepar-able. When I had to fight to get more money for my production of the *Marat/Sade*, Ian was my ally at an extraordinary general meeting of DramSoc. When, in the summer holidays, I took a job in a pea-canning factory in Peterborough, Ian came with me, and we worked fourteen hours a day pitchforking pea plants into a machine and shared a boarding-house with a Yugoslavian fork-lift operator. The management there operated a con bonus system, trying to get the different gangs of men to compete as to who could manage the greatest tonnage of peas. And Ian and I went from gang to gang trying to persuade them not to bother, without much success.

Then, later that summer, we shared a flat in Edinburgh and appeared in *Mandrake*, a musical, at the festival, in which Ian played the hero. He had a wonderful voice. I suspect that if he

[51]

had chosen to train it, he could have had a career as a singer.

That was the pattern of those summers: taking a job for a few weeks, acting in the festival and then, inevitably we'd have failed our end-of-year exams, so after the festival when Edinburgh would empty, we'd have an awful couple of weeks getting ready for re-sits.

We met up again in London – I'd already spent a year at RADA – when Ian went to LAMDA. We shared flats again, neither of us having grants and both being very short of money. We lived for a time in a flat in Belgravia owned by a Turk called Cenghis. Then, for a year we slept on the floor of Peter and Marylyn Johnstone's flat in North Finchley. Peter and Marylyn were at university with us and remained good friends – Ian's cat, Bradley, now lives with them in Somerset. Despite the lack of money, once a month we would all chip in five pounds and Marylyn would cook us a gourmet meal, normally followed by a game of bridge. Ian was an enthusiastic, if maddeningly slow, bridge player.

I think we both missed the freedom we'd had at DramSoc of having control over our work, but Ian loved being a drama student. He was a golden boy at LAMDA, just as he'd been in Edinburgh. Afterwards I used to think they could have challenged him more. Ian had a wonderful facility for making acting look easy and perhaps in the early days teachers and directors could have been more rigorous with him.

We never worked together professionally. I wish we had. At one time, Ian suggested that I might direct him in a production of *Hamlet*, but nothing came of it. We didn't often go up for the same parts together and though there was some rivalry between us – naturally enough, both being ambitious and both coming from a similar background – it wasn't a destructive rivalry. I spent a lot of time working outside London and quite long periods could pass without my seeing him. But that never seemed to matter. I wouldn't want it to seem that there was only a beginning and an end to our friendship. But it's hard to know what to say about the middle period. It's hard to know what to say about any of it, really.

I remember ... Ian coming back from India where they'd been filming *Gandhi* and being full of stories, talking and talking about it, delighted by India's mixture of the brutally practical and the fantastic. He'd made lots of friends there and brought back a selection of lungis — loincloths — that he used to wear about the house.

And I remember a night in Edinburgh when I was appearing in *The Thrie Estaites*. After the show Ian, his parents and I sat drinking after closing hours with a group of Scots actors in the back room of a pub off the Royal Mile. We all got up and sang songs and recited poems — Ian sang 'My Love is Like a Red, Red Rose' and 'The Twa Corbies'. A wonderfully Scottish night, part of the Scottish tradition of people with a couple of drinks under their belts getting up and doing a turn, a tradition that Ian was absolutely part of.

Being Scottish was very important to Ian. He never lost his Scots accent. Not that he tortured himself with aggressive Scottishness, but he didn't seek to anglicize himself either. He simply accepted that being Scots was an important part of who he was. He had an honest individuality. He came from a remarkable family, parents with strong socialist principles. Ian had that socialist streak too and he never lost it.

There was a time — what an irony it seems now — when I wondered how it would be for Ian as a middle-aged actor, because he had a youthful, slightly Peter Pan-ish quality about

[53]

him. But towards the end of his career he became better and better and deeper as an actor. A new sort of solidity came through in *Fool for Love* and *Cat on a Hot Tin Roof*. And then there was his Hamlet. But I couldn't be objective about that.

A lot of Ian's last year was effort: deciding whether to do Hamlet and then finding the energy to do it. Hamlet was an extraordinary focus for him. Towards the end I suppose he focused down from larger worries onto specifics – like the swelling of his face.

I used to go to his flat most days when he was very ill. I usually did the cooking. Not an easy patient, he could be incredibly generous and equally difficult: very particular about how his porridge was made and furious if it wasn't right. He was also very brave, fighting for his independence right to the end. He didn't want to stay in hospital. He carried on driving his car for as long as he possibly could. Constantly he was questioning the treatments of conventional medicine and trying out other methods, wanting to be in control of what was done to him. A week before he died, he was furiously ordering paints and brushes. He wanted to finish off one of his paintings.

He didn't go quietly. He was incredibly tenacious of life.

I didn't talk to him much towards the end about death or his fears or any spiritual matters. In a way we didn't say very much. But I don't feel the lack of it. We reached some kind of understanding. We didn't really need to talk. And when he died I didn't feel anything was left unsaid between us. He had achieved a strange sort of serenity, I think.

RUBY WAX

THE best time of my life – besides summer camp – was in Stratford when I was with the RSC and I met Ian. I saw Stratford through gold. Since then the idealism has been knocked out of me, but then I believed I'd arrived. (For an American the RSC is synonymous with meeting God.) Ian was the source of it all. I just saw a golden haze and that golden boy.

I first met Ian at a garden party in Stratford with my mother. When my mother saw him her breath was taken away. He was the most beautiful man she'd ever seen, 'a young Robert Redford' (the ultimate compliment). My mother said: 'That's the one that's going to be famous.' And she was right for once. Ian was beautiful – and then he opened his mouth and I discovered his stunning sense of humour. I'd never seen anyone score a double-header like that.

I went into the RSC at the lowest level. I played a piece of seaweed in *The Tempest*. Ian was Ariel. The play was done on a garbage bag representing timelessness. The production didn't have a chance. In the middle of this mess Ian was lowered from the ceiling and he sang. For those few minutes he created something brilliant. For a year, every night the chills would go up my back. I'd never heard a voice like it. I won't remember him looking the way he did at the end – always the way he did then. I'll have that image of him as Ariel above me, with his face glowing. And hearing that voice. Such a raunchy boy with the voice of an angel.

We were also in *The Taming of the Shrew*. I watched Ian night after night saying the lines he made his. Everybody else was acting their parts but Ian just did his. He could say complicated verse and make it sound as earthed as someone giving a gardening demo. Because of Ian I finally understood why Shakespeare was funny. (Up until then I thought it was a rumour.) With a tiny inflection, Ian could give a line a thousand innuendos.

Mortals don't meet people like him. At Stratford he had a kind of cult following. Girls were excited. So were men. This is James Dean territory. Ian sent out a kind of thrill which he was unaware of.

And just when you thought you'd come to the end of his talents, he would sit up all night playing the piano. He could do rock'n'roll with his friend Hilton that made your hair stand on end.

Ian went along with all my antics. While at Stratford, I'd organize horrible outings for the company. He was always there to tell me I'd screwed up. The Galloping Gaucho – a hideous Mexican restaurant at the back of a bed and breakfast with sombreros covering the walls – was definitely the lowest of my social endeavours. And Ian was faithfully there, smirking at me. But he watched over me too. I think he saw me as an underdog, which I was at the time.

[58]

We didn't become friends right away. As a matter of fact he rejected me. I was just a novice piece of seaweed, don't forget. Most of my energy was not about getting successful but about getting to know Ian. It took me a whole season to claw my way into his attention range. Eventually, when we had a break I begged him to come to my Miami with me.

Ian stayed at my parents' apartment in Miami. When he went to the pool you saw very old women literally back-bend because he was so stunning. He just sat there, a bronzed god, while they lined up and gave him the goods about their life. He told great stories about it afterwards, imitating them perfectly. They appealed to his sense of kitsch. Charlotte who wore her wealth up and down her arm: a bracelet for each husband. And Dorothy, who'd had a silicone injection in her face so the only things that moved were the tips of her lips. She came up to him and said: 'You see that window up there? My husband jumped out of it and I don't give a shit.'

His wit was so accurate, so observant. He could pierce right through any façade. I've seen him take over a room, telling these great stories. He'd have people screaming.

We had the same sense of what was funny. With us it was a kind of flirtatiousness. I'd give it to him and he'd give it back. Instead of sex he'd give that out, which is better than sex – ask any woman. (A man who makes you laugh as hard as that leaves everything else limp.) I've only met a couple of men like that in my life. Ian was so observant about me. He would lovingly rip me to shreds. To me, when done with affection, that's the ultimate flattery.

Ian pointed out quite early on that I was a terrible classical actress. But when I started doing my own comedy shows, he

[59]

was always there. When I finally started to make him laugh, I knew I was on the right track.

He could be wild. Once we went up to Liverpool – I had a small part with him in *Chariots of Fire*. When we got to the Adelphi Hotel, the Royal Ballet was there and we coerced them into swimming in the pool. They all ended up completely naked and I choreographed a hideous water ballet. Ian loved things like that and would encourage me – he was too Scottish to actually do them himself. He could bring out the best in people.

I never cried with Ian. It wasn't that kind of friendship. But I wouldn't want him to sound like some kind of superficial one-liner-merchant. I knew he was deep. To be that amusing you have to go deep deep into yourself. You need a creative intelligence to be so observant. His cold controlled Scottish protestant façade on the outside and inside this . . . creature. Just a little bit more to the right and Ian would have been an upstanding citizen. A loose gene made him go wild.

And there was a bit of Ian that was just the housewife who loved to go round the corner and get a cabbage. He would make you dinner and be like a homespun, Scottish widow.

His dry way of responding was very Scottish. And part of his sexiness. A repressed man – and underneath something hot. You'd feel like you were playing footsy with him to kick up the motors. And then a great spirit was released.

He used to hug me a lot. I think I was like a younger sister to him. Once I went with him up to his parents' place. I begged them to adopt me, so I could be nearer to Ian – I knew marriage was out.

After *Chariots*, Ian's career should have taken off. He should have been a really big success. Perhaps he was too honest for the film business. That kind of honesty can be disturbing.

There was nobody as talented as he was. The theatrical contribution that he could have made . . . It would have broken all the rules. When everybody else was acting their socks off, Ian would stroll on, cool, with the minimum amount of energy, because he knew what he was. When I was splitting my guts trying to be funny, Ian would clean up with just a look out of the corner of his eye.

I didn't see him as much as I should have over the years when we were both in London. I should have been running after him a lot more. He was the star in our relationship.

When he was sick, he kept it to himself. He'd always say he had sinus problems. Perhaps he didn't want people looking at him with pity. In the end when I visited him at home, of course I knew, but we didn't really discuss it. He didn't like to wallow. I think he resolved coming to terms with death. He went through his journey. And he always kept that spark.

I wish I could be more specific about how funny this man was. It was really exciting to be around his presence. There's never been anyone else like him in my life. He was the thrill. He was it.

SHARMAN MACDONALD

I met him first on top of a 26 bus, in Edinburgh, down by
the Bridges, when I was sixteen. I've been a worshipper ever
since. It was the night he left the Royal High. 'I'm terribly
sorry,' he said. 'I'm afraid I'm drunk.' I didn't say anything very
much. It's no good being a worshipper. Kills the conversation
stone dead.

Portobello nights. Late night buses. After rehearsals. Walking
along the sea-front with the haar rolling in from the sea. Freezing
to death. *Edward II* was the first thing we did together. And
David. And Hilton too.* Ian was Gaveston, I was Isabelle. He
was magic, I was not. 'Farewell base stooping to the lordly peers'
sent tingles up my spine. 'That boy,' my mother said, 'that boy
held the audience in the palm of his hand. That boy has what it
takes.' Then she looked at me. 'Why did you turn your back on
the audience?' Kindly, she said, 'Why did you say all your lines
into the curtain? Why did you do that?'

An afternoon at Restalrig Road. In the front room where the
piano was. Ian's painting a picture of a group of old men leaning
on sticks, standing up on Arthur's Seat. Tones of sepia. Oil on

* David Rintoul and Hilton McRae.

[65]

canvas. The cat's in the room. A big ginger tom, Mephistopheles by name. I'm watching Ian paint. Bare arms. Hand curved round the brush like a back-handed writer. White arm. Broad strong hand.

Evenings he'd spend designing clothes for me and Chris Daw. Impossible garments. Wild metallic things with bare patches here and there. And he'd seriously explain to us that we really ought to wear them.

Nights of charades. Long quotations from novels, preferably Russian, painstakingly played out.

'Can I drive?' We're in my father's Triumph Herald. It's night-time in Joppa. The widest road in Joppa. Ian wants to practise three point turns. I let him. We swop seats. 'Gently,' I say. 'Gently.' Ian puts his foot down. The car whizzes straight back into a lamp post. My father's car. Working on the falling off a bike principle, get straight back on, that principle, 'Try again,' I say. He pulls the car forward. 'Well done,' I say. Puts the car into reverse. Puts his foot down and whizzes straight back into the lamp post again. My father's car.

A party at the bungalow. My parents are abroad. Corn beef mashed up in a scallop shell. Ian's standing there all alone in the dining-room. Waves his fork in the air. Chews thoughtfully. 'Very good,' he says. 'Very good.' Raises a devil's eyebrow. 'Crab is it?' Later he sang 'Ae Fond Kiss' and 'Fanette' unaccompanied, making music out of silence, going into silence.

St Giles Cathedral. The Watch Night Service. Standing beside Ian, listening to him sing. Doing the Christmas post. Queuing up to be paid. Him getting more than me. Because then men did. Me speechless, furious, because I didn't know until that moment, that very moment, innocent that I was, that men were deemed to be worth more than women. Drives down to Gullane.

[66]

The wind whipping the sand up off the dunes. Hot sweet tea in the kitchen at Restalrig Road. Cutting Ian's hair at the bungalow. 'It's not even,' I say. 'Cut some more off,' he says. 'It's still not even,' I'm getting desperate now. Ian's long silky blond hair's lying all over the floor. But he's laughing. 'Cut it shorter,' he says. 'Cut it shorter.' The smell of French cigarettes.

There came a day of lethargy for me. Lethargy induced by defeat. 1971 this was. Ian was already at LAMDA. I wanted to go into the theatre. My whole family was against it. Not just the parents. My uncle was vociferous in his objections. Six foot four, my uncle. A man of devastating wit. A good man, eloquent on the subject of duty. They had won, all of them. Ian and Steph Feyerman had come up to do a children's show. The end of the festival, this was. In the George Square Theatre. After the show I was sitting there on the stairs half-way up the auditorium. Ian stepped down off the stage. Climbed up. Stood above me.

'Are you going to drama college?' he said. I shrugged my shoulders. 'For fuck sake get your finger out.' He turned and walked away. A tall figure in black, coming back from another world, telling me to do what I wanted. Giving me permission. Giving me support.

I talk about him when I can. As if some of his magic will return in fact rather than in memory if I say his name often enough. Ian Charleson. I don't know what that magic was. I can't define it, nail it down. I wish I could. His singing. His laughter. His grace. I drank in his performances. They were my inspiration. His beauty. Brick in *Cat on a Hot Tin Roof*. The wit and spirit of that last Hamlet. And the pain. He was a wonderful actor. He was a man I loved. I miss him.

[67]

J.G. Farrell's *Troubles* ith Emer Gillespie, for levision, 1988.

Codename Kyril, a spy riller for television, 1988.

Above: As Brick in Howard Davies' production of *Cat on a Hot Tin Roof* at the National. *Below left*: with Lindsay Duncan as Margaret. *Right*: Rehearsing for Richard Eyre's production of *Hamlet* at the National, 1989.

Opposite: Portrait, August 1989 by Johnny Rozsa.

Overleaf: Photographed for the *Hamlet* poster by Johnny Rozsa, 1988.

Oxbridge Blues by Frederick Raphael for television, 1984.

In Sidney Sheldon's *Master of the Game* for television, 1983.

'Royal Night of a Hundred Stars' on LWT, 31 March 1985.

In the back garden with Hilton McRae and David Rintoul.

Left: New York, Christmas 1986. *Right*: With Philip Sayer, New York, Christmas 1986.

With Sean Mathias, Morocco, 1986.

Overleaf: Photographed for *Car Trouble* (1986) with Julie Walters by Johnny Rozsa.

RICHARD WARWICK

I AN was an artist. I mean, he wasn't merely a fine actor, he was a musician, a singer, a painter, a gardener and a great wit.

He had the most wonderful sense of the absurd. He enjoyed nothing more than having an audience round a table and reducing any situation to the point of ridicule. I don't mean he was a 'big' 'Oscar Wilde' kind of a wit. His was a much quieter, more innocent sort of waggishness.

God, he was fun.

He also drove me mad. Any decision was impossible for him. If we were going to a movie, I had to decide on the film, the time, the place, when to meet, what to do afterwards – everything. But that was part of his attraction, and maybe we all enjoyed bossing him around.

He suffered a lot too. He resented the fact that his film career never came to more; but then if it had, he'd probably never have had his successes in the theatre.

Ian never had a lover. He was often quite lonely. He would always say, 'Well, isn't that the human condition, after all?' Perhaps he was right.

His illness was wretched. He was terrified. We were all terrified.

And I miss him just as much as I knew I would.

JOHANNA KIRBY

THE first time I met Ian was at an actors' workshop. He reminded me of a blond angel. After we danced around the room a bit, I thought he's definitely a fallen one, because he has the wickedest glint in his eye. During this exercise called 'In Imagination' Ian was to ask me to dance and then go home with him. 'Chance would be a fine thing,' I thought. Of course even in the exercise we never got that far. We both collapsed laughing.

Then we shared a house for three years in Beauclerc Road, Hammersmith owned by Simon Crowther. The bathroom overlooked everybody's back garden. It was a very peaceful room with beautiful conches around the bath. 'Can you hear the sea in yours Jo?' I remember him asking.

'Yes,' I said. 'Yes I can.'

I never went into Ian's bedroom without being asked except when he hadn't surfaced for three days with migraine. There were times he would call me into his room to listen to a piece of music he particularly liked. He'd sigh, catching his breath. I found this very attractive, simply because music was important to him and he wanted to share it. He taught me a lot about music and how to listen to it.

He worked very hard to get himself into shape for *Chariots of Fire*. He drank a horrible looking white concoction full of vitamins for breakfast and bicycled everywhere. It was a time of great confidence for him and these memories make my acceptance of his death all the more difficult.

I remember sitting in the garden with him at one o'clock in the morning. He said he'd like to play Liddell in *Chariots* because the part would fit like a kid glove. He loved the way his character ran, arms and legs flaying. There was something very sensual in it which was in Ian too, I felt. He said he didn't think he'd ever have the sort of faith that would refuse to run the Olympics on the Sabbath. 'I haven't either,' I said. 'You'll just have to get the oil-can out, darling . . . drip . . . drip and use your imagination.'

He was invited to lots of parties. At one, he sat next to Lady Falkender whom he liked, much to his surprise. They were both socialists and Ian gave considerable amounts of money to further the political causes he believed in. He was very consistent in his beliefs. Success did not change this.

Ian used to sing in the bath. His beautiful voice only irritated me when I was in a hurry. One morning he let me in so I could quickly brush my teeth and get out. We caught sight of each other in the mirror. We both looked jaded. (We'd been up half the night playing cards.) He told me that there were blown up photographs of him all around Bloomingdale's cosmetic department and *this* was what he really looked like. We were lost laughing at the awful trick that was being played on people. He was great fun.

I did see *Hamlet*. When Ian came on stage I didn't recognize him. His face was swollen and I couldn't see his eyes. Those

[76]

sitting behind me kept saying, 'Is it him?' 'Is it really him?' This was the first time I felt the loneliness of his situation. And yet what courage and great acting was on display. He seemed completely self-possessed. He brought his thoughts and his feelings together and offered them to the audience with clarity, intelligence and grace. I felt so much respect for him. But how could I tell a man dying of AIDS, that in the end, this situation was all so life-embracing for everybody? In the bar later all I could do was throw my arms around him. I said, 'I'm sorry. I don't have any words at the moment.' He smiled with great affection. He then asked me bluntly, 'Did you notice . . . ?' and gestured to his face.

'Yes,' I said. And then it became ordinary and didn't matter. 'Let's go and eat,' he said and we talked for two hours and went home at one in the morning.

The last time I saw him was Xmas Day at a party. He was wearing a tartan waistcoat, another 'celebration'. When I sat next to him, at one point he rubbed my knee with his hand and I thought at the time, 'This is what I should be doing, for him.' However, in the end, I see this as an affirmation of something – something I don't yet quite understand, an example or sign of his deep generosity.

PETER EYRE

I T was the early seventies, and we used to go to a crowded basement club in Jermyn Street after the show. One night my colleague Susan Fleetwood pointed out a young man dressed in white, darting from table to table, group to group: 'That's the boy I told you about. He just had a terrible time doing *Hamlet*.' A friend of hers had directed a touring production of *Hamlet*. The director was experienced, the Hamlet, relatively inexperienced but very gifted. Apparently, it just didn't work. I had recently done the part, and had not exactly set the Thames on fire. I felt a comradely twinge of sympathy for this other disappointed *Hamlet*.

That's when I first saw Ian Charleson. I think we exchanged mutual self-deprecating critiques of our performances, our productions. Nothing too serious. It is obvious that Hamlet is an enormously demanding role technically, but it is also psychologically taxing. More than any other role, it requires from the actor a deep exploration of self, the true self, to get anywhere near the emotional scale of the character. Most people who attempt it, successfully or unsuccessfully, find the personal aspects of the role extremely painful and daunting. A failure in this part leaves

[81]

one with both the bitter realization that one is not technically up to it, and the very private despair of not finding within oneself the depth of feeling to make the part live. It can be like a too speedy psychoanalysis which stirs up all the unconscious worlds, and ends in leaving the patient confused and adrift. I remember the experience making me feel quite bananas.

In the smoky nightclub, Ian managed to convey similar thoughts. He also had felt bananas. However, the subject of *Hamlet* was only lightly touched upon. We hadn't gone to a nightclub to discuss the classics.

Later, when I got to know Ian, I sometimes heard him refer to that *Hamlet*, but only in passing and with that sense of comic outrage appropriate for theatrical 'turkeys'. I loved his acerbic wit and his humorous railings against the world. Without ever becoming a close friend, I got to know him well, and enjoyed that kind of friendship based on professional familiarity and respect (or maybe even lack of respect), a kind of intimacy where, after not seeing each other for a long period, you run into each other, and with some intensity exchange personal and professional confidences, which lead to nothing more than doing exactly the same again when you meet two years later.

In the theatre and on the big screen I admired him greatly, most especially in *Cat on a Hot Tin Roof* where he rose to new heights and gave a deeply felt and powerful performance as Brick, always thought to be an almost impossible part. I thought he was definitive.

When I heard that Ian was doing *Hamlet* again and had opened at the National Theatre, I went along to a matinée. Just as I was about to go into the auditorium I saw a notice saying the understudy was to play at this performance. My heart sank, and I went home wondering what had happened. A friend upbraided me on the telephone: 'How the hell do you expect him to do two *Hamlets* in one day? Use your head, dear. It's extraordinary he can do it once. Two months ago he wouldn't have got through ten minutes of the play.'

A week later I went again. I don't expect ever to see the part better played. From the moment of his first entrance and his first line, said in that light but perfectly placed tenor, you knew you were in the presence of a great artist. The shock of his altered appearance, his face disfigured by illness, soon became almost insignificant. The detail of his work, every line profoundly felt, every speech beautifully modulated (he had always been a natural verse speaker) was so prodigious I found myself drawn into the secret world of Hamlet as never before. It was almost as if he had been able to use his physical liability in some mysterious way as an advantage, so that an audience which would have at an earlier time looked at Hamlet the Prince, the handsome and noble Ian Charleson, were now encouraged to look *into* Hamlet the Prince, another Ian Charleson, transformed by suffering, forced to contemplate the end of life.

I have never felt the spiritual side of Hamlet so strongly. Two moments stand out. When he said, 'O all ye host of heaven', he threw his arms wide open to the skies, as if addressing and embracing the cosmos, a gesture he told me, in his typically self-deprecating way, he had 'stolen' from a painting he had seen of a nineteenth-century tragedian. Whatever its genesis, this gesture was integral to his performance, and showed his determination to meet the metaphysical dimension of the play, just as he had challenged his own mortality with defiance and bravado by attempting the role at this point in his life. When later in the play Hamlet says to Horatio, 'We defy augury. There is special providence in the fall of a sparrow' (the second unforgettable moment which makes me shiver as I recall it), I felt I was experiencing the tragedy of *Hamlet* as if for the first time. I have only once before (in Michael Redgrave's Uncle Vanya) had this almost mystical feeling in a theatre of watching an actor become so totally the role he is playing there is no discernible gap between him and the character.

Every now and then during the play, my involuntary memory would unkindly remind me of my early hesitant effort at Hamlet, a line reading, a move, a little moment, as if while watching Ian I was being pointedly reminded what it is to undertake such a role, what skill and humility you need to take even the first steps, and how my dismal failure was somehow being generously extinguished in my regretful memory, now that I had the privilege of witnessing the perfecting of the role. I was learning a lesson in acting you can never learn too well. However great the preparation, the exploration of self, the energy and skill, you can always act better. Ian had 'acted better'. I wondered now what that early Hamlet had been like, the Hamlet of a vigorous and beautiful young man. Did he have to suffer so much to become the great Hamlet he now became? I suppose the answer is – yes.

Dear Ian, you taught us a lesson in life, and a lesson in art.

JOHN WHITWORTH

Speak Thou, Boy

A' shall not tread on me!
I'll run away till I'm bigger, but then I'll fight

Dead now, and three years junior to me,
Young Charleson. Though your trade, like mine, was
    words,
I see you in an early, one line part,
Freckled, with pale, straight hair, Coriolanus' son.
He roared the verse with some authority
(His father was Town Clerk of Haddington)
Till, changing cardboard spears for wooden swords,
We stabbed the prefect bastard to the heart.

One greaseball smoker, actorishly inclined,
Without your talent, confidence or looks,
Enjoyed your chat and cheerfully dirty mind:
The stage was your ice-cream as mine is books.
You played the end with dignity, they said.
But not too much, I hope.

                              I'm sad you're dead.

[87]

SEAN MATHIAS

I N Morocco, the land of sorcery and exotic flirtation, in a
small hotel nestling south of the Atlas, a seductive stone's
throw from the desert and its impending mystery, Ian looked
at me across the dining table and said, 'I suppose I'd like to tell
you this. I've got the HIV virus.'

A close friend of mine had recently died of AIDS in America
and I knew several other Americans who had died or were dying.
But this was the moment I had been expecting and dreading:
someone on my very own British doorstep with the virus in their
system.

I first met Ian Charleson fourteen years ago in London in the
long hot summer of 1976. He belonged to a rare group of
glamorous, witty and urbane fellows including the actor Philip
Sayer, the photographer Johnny Rosza and the fashion designer
Rifat Ozbek. They peacocked their way through the city talking
a unique language. Terms of endearment took the form 'Mum'
and 'Toast'. Nothing so essentially faggy as 'My dear' or 'Darling.' 'It's a fierce day Toast.' 'Love the new hair-do Mum.'
The words contorted into their own strange speech patterns, a
childish idiosyncrasy invented by these high priests of fashion.

If a question was in any way rhetorical the response would be 'Pope!' with that compulsory exclamation mark. This was, naturally, an abbreviation of 'Is the Pope Catholic?' Ian always seemed paradoxically to be a part of this ritual whilst remaining independent. He rode a bicycle where others walked, swam at Marshall Street Baths as opposed to the trendier Oasis, yet he appeared in successful runs of West End plays, numbered amongst his friends luminaries like Alan Bates or Ian McKellen, dined with Vanessa Redgrave, was rumoured to be screwing a glamorous, unnamed actress. He was tricky to define. I was the novice. Without the confidence to utter their strange, harrowing, completely handsome language. Was Ian Charleson attractive? Pope! Was I intimidated by him? Pope!

Slowly, over the years, I started to know Ian better and grew to like and admire him. It seemed we had one thing in common, when the partying was in full swing and the screaming had really started we could sit quietly in some corner and have a heart to heart. He enjoyed a good time as much as, no more than, the next guy but he also possessed the ability to observe and analyse, to stand back and rationalize life. It was this quality which led him through his illness.

When his Scottish nous failed him he would become depressed, passive, unable to make the simplest decision. When he stayed sharp he was inspired, as witty as Wilde, as wild and handsome as Clift, as bright as any of his peers and more fun than most.

Although Ian was nearly seven years older than me, my role was to become that of elder brother, listener and adviser. He took a risk in telling me his secret news on our Moroccan trip – he was not only relying on my discretion but even more substantially on my understanding of the situation. The whole issue of HIV is a complicated one and in 1986 it was still early days for assessing the problem. At that time I hadn't even considered taking an HIV test and in my darker moments, which were frequent, considered it a strong possibility that I had the virus. Ian would have thought about all this before potentially burdening me. This was another quality of his; an almost lawyer-like brain that would think globally around every problem.

When confronted with this alarming news I did not stop to ponder Ian's death. The subject of dying was one we avoided. Our relationship was about life and, more than anyone I have ever known, he proved that life is about attacking under adversity. Although he referred on several occasions to suicide, staying in the ring was more his style and no victory could have been more public and simultaneously more personal and intensely private than his exploration of life and death through his portrayal of Hamlet. A spiritual labyrinth consisting of the hunt for truth, it became the symbolic climax of his life. And I begged him not to tackle the part. In a sea of encouragement I was the lone, strong voice of dissent, because I feared for his health. But apart from the spiritual and moral journey he made with Hamlet, it was a particularly fortuitous end to a career which in many ways had left him dissatisfied in recent years. Following *Chariots of Fire*, Ian the paradox had found himself trapped in the desire to become the stuff Hollywood dreams are made of, a matinée idol thrusting his assumed heterosexuality onto our cinema screens, and the conflicting need to pursue a rich theatrical career spanning the heroes of Shakespeare.

Whilst here was an actor who could please on stage or screen his career had started to somewhat pervert itself in the pursuit of two opposing routes. Linked inextricably to all of this was the person behind the personae, and converging on the struggle for his 'real' status as a leading actor was his struggle of coming to terms with being gay. Just as Ian appeared to be more and more relaxed about his gayness, into the arena had been thrown the punishing reality of his HIV status. It arrived in his life when he might have been blossoming fully in the acceptance of his sexuality, but he now had to deal with the potential onslaught of full-blown AIDS, and the necessity to spend a lot of energy attempting to block that onslaught. He embraced alternative medicine, the holistic approach and the belief that physical exercise supports the immune system, with the same dedication with which he approached his professional life.

Ian's struggle was intense and the day at the beginning of 1989 he told me that full-blown AIDS had erupted in his body just weeks earlier, was a devastating one. In spite of this our relationship was endlessly informed by humour and laughter. We mocked the world together and laughed at the most shocking and frightening events; most importantly not in others but in our own lives. It is this laughter that I miss. We travelled away together, returned to Morocco, went to New York, made day trips, parties, dinners. Ian was a wonderful cook and I always loved the easygoing atmosphere round at his Hammersmith flat which led onto an abundant garden. His converted back yard could have won prizes. He attached great importance to organic growth and tended and treated his flora with the patience of a kindly parent.

His discontent, sometimes boring incessant moaning, was directed at his career, not his HIV status, nor later at his full-blown AIDS. His envy of other, often less talented though heavily lionized actors was occasionally a stumbling block. It was my

impatience with this self-lacerating, self-imprisoning attitude
that emboldened me to offer him the role of Greta when I first
directed *Bent*, Martin Sherman's play concerning the persecution
of homosexuals in Nazi Germany. Greta is a drag artist who
draws a veil over his own sexuality in order to survive Nazism.
A tough businessman with a gutter tongue. The notion of
helping Ian Charleson into fishnets and advising on mascara was
irresistible. That would really give him something to moan
about. Greta was also required to sing and Ian had a heavenly
voice.

More importantly *Bent* was being staged, in full production
for one performance only, to raise money for Stonewall, a group
being set up to lobby on behalf of lesbians and gay men and to
fight prejudice and harassment. Anyone appearing on the bill,
and it was completely star-studded, was declaring themselves,
regardless of their sexuality, to be a supporter of the gay movement.

But the most gargantuan part of it all, from Ian's point of
view, was that here was a man with AIDS, his torso now covered
by karposi sarcoma, his face starting to distort and disfigure,
dressed convincingly as a glamorous and roguish Dietrich-
type woman, and the secret behind that portrayal was that
he, the director and the costume designer were the only people
connected with the production who knew about his illness. Naturally there were rumours but people didn't know the
facts.

During the technical rehearsal at the Adelphi Theatre Ian
started to question his entrance from the song into the scene, set
in Greta's dressing-room. He was to change during the scene
from full drag Greta, into the bitter, Scottish, wisecracking club
owner. This meant a full change of costume in front of the

[95]

audience. Woman to Man. We had rehearsed the details of the scene very thoroughly in the rehearsal room but things often go through vast unexplained differences when they reach a stage. Ian wasn't exactly making a fuss but seemed, from my position in the middle of the circle, to be dithering about. It later transpired that anyone in the wings could see his bare back and although there was a screen set on stage for Ian to periodically drift behind, the stage-hands would still be able to see his skin and possibly detect the marks on it which were KS. Another actor under this pressure might have panicked, might understandably have become neurotic and delayed the hideously tight schedule, but Ian decided to get on with it, let the matter drop, played the scene exactly as rehearsed. He was gently nudging toward telling the world he had AIDS. The man was a hero. And he received a hero's welcome that night at the curtain call. The sheer intensity of the sound that greeted Charleson's walk-down on the Adelphi stage was deafening. The cliché, the roar of the crowd, would be completely inadequate. They welcomed him like some great god who'd come amongst them. It was at one and the same time uplifting and utterly tragic.

An instinctive premonition of the loss the theatrical community was to suffer. I lost a mate, Ian's family lost their beloved boy and the world of the arts lost a gifted, complicated, highly-charged, creative man.

Fighting with the cut glass of his own hour-time,
A warrior swooped down with fierce tread and nimble feet.
Agile in the land of spiralling Fate, he strode about
in the glorious heat of his perfection.

[96]

Friend, brother, son and lover, a careless smile, a careful
  wit.
A wilful child unlike no other, with mocking brain,
giant pace, delicate heart and angel face.
Smiling shyly at the slyly changing edge of the moon,
a song to sing, a boy of cheer who lost the tune.

Battling man with laser nerve,
a razor tongue to cut the cost of his own ill.
Challenging Life and its substantial lies.
Forging on with iron will, he fought like a master,
taught like a hero, claimed Victory in simple truth.
Passing by in urgent flight, there goes a friend who'll never
  fade.

CATRIONA CRAIG

(from a letter)

. . . I went to see *Hamlet* again with a very strange looking Ian Charleson playing the Dane. Very strange looking because he has just had a synus operation which has left his face very puffy. (One gets these little snippets of information if one reads the *Guardian* carefully.) Anyway he completely saved an otherwise stale production with his amazing performance. He made every single line personal and meaningful. I felt as if I had a very close friend who was desperately unhappy and who had come to tell me how he was feeling. Because he was little, weedy and ugly he seemed to be completely at odds with this violent masculine world that he had to conform to. He was a hundred times more articulate and sensitive than any of the other characters and for this reason he was suffering. Nearly every time he appeared he was carrying a book – not in a studious way but in a rebellious way – as if he was saying 'I hereby declare that the pen is mightier than the sword.'

During the lines about 'Villain, damned smiling villain', he actually got out a pen and scribbled down the words – as if words were all he could put his faith in.

I couldn't bear the death scene. Once he knew that he had

been poisoned he simply walked across to Horatio saying 'I am dead,' not knowing what to do. How do you spend your last minute of life? He looked completely numb — and when he finally died he just relaxed into Horatio's arms. He laid him down, curled up in the foetal position saying 'Good night sweet Prince,' as if he was putting a child to bed. I bawled my eyes out. In fact I didn't altogether stop crying until I was in Waterloo Station. *Hamlet* is now *strongly recommended.* . . .

SUZANNE BERTISH

O N the night I went to see Ian's Hamlet at the National
there were a lot of sixth-formers in the theatre who
can be a lousy audience, but from the first soliloquy
Ian captured them. At the end nearly everyone rose to their
feet and cheered, something I've never seen at a Shakespeare
performance at the RSC or the National. That was an audience
unifying. It's a very powerful thing. And Ian did that. Even if
people didn't really know what was being touched on, something
very deep and primeval had happened.

Ian rehearsed and performed Hamlet while he was dying. It
seemed to me that he shared with the audience, through 'Hamlet', the extraordinary and unimaginable journey that he had
been on from the start of a devastating disease. So, with a noble
heart and generous spirit, he played the part, not with showy
pyrotechnics, but with great clarity and simplicity and truth. I
don't expect I'll ever see Hamlet so profoundly performed again.

Ian was always very honest about the productions he was in
and about the work he was doing. He wouldn't pretend something was wonderful when it wasn't. I found that very exciting
and refreshing. A lot of actors and directors are blind to their

work. The business is littered with misplaced egos and phoneys. But Ian had an incisive overview. He could have been a director. Watching one of his performances you would find he was completely committed, immersed in it. But afterwards he could say: this is wrong with it, that is wrong with it. He would never let go of trying to get to the truth. I think you pay a huge price for being as honest as Ian was. It causes you a lot of pain.

It would be in about 1974 or 1975 when I first met Ian. It was in Devon. I suppose Ian must have come down to see David Rintoul who was on tour with me. I just remember the sunlight and the rich, lush countryside and Ian being so attractive. Later on in London we became friends. We'd meet at parties and at plays. I always felt I had an affinity with him. Maybe that had something to do with our birthdays being close together and us both being Leos. I always felt I could pick up the phone, even after months and months, and have a chat and that he would understand what I was feeling.

I worked with Ian at the Theatre Museum the year before he died. We did a reading of *Macbeth*. He was wonderful to work with, remarkable for his lack of ego. It was a collaborative process, which is the way it ought to be. He realized that nobody knows all the answers. So we could share ideas. He'd have ideas about my part and I'd have ideas about his. So many English actors are all head, but Ian had a really good balance: fiercely intelligent, but also very intuitive.

I don't cry easily, but Ian as an actor made me cry three times: in *Chariots of Fire*, in *Gandhi* and in *Hamlet*.

I spoke to Ian a lot in the last year of his life. I probably saw him more consistently then than I'd ever seen him in previous years. We would talk about our friend Philip Sayer who was dying of cancer. And sometimes we talked about alternative medicine – the holistic view. Mostly our conversations were quite down to earth, but a few times they went beyond that. There was definitely a kind of understanding between us. He was sharing something with me which he thought I could hear. He would refer to black, troubled times he'd been through. He had plunged to the depths in order to have a greater understanding.

Ian always had a wonderful clarity. It was part of his nature. But towards the end it was a quality he had to a heightened and deepened degree. That blazing honesty. He was one of those people who look right through you and know. He saw things exactly for what they were.

He had a very compressed amount of time to do all his living – and he did it. I couldn't be sure, but I feel there was a sort of roundedness to his life. That's very inspiring.

So much garbage is written about AIDS being the wrath of God. I think it's important to go towards the disease and not back away from it because AIDS belongs to everybody. It's such a part of the world we live in. It is a breakdown of the immune system. And our planet's immune system has also been broken down. Our generation hasn't lived through a war. The generation who did live through a war knew that their young men were going off to fight for world freedom, to fight the fascist movement. But this is like a war. Some of our young men – like Ian – have been chosen to battle it out on the front line. They are sacrificed, for us. We have to look inside ourselves and try to become whole. You change, the world changes.

I miss him. I miss the chats, the wit, the take on life. So many encounters when I would hoot and roar with laughter. Often, I could share with him how I was really feeling about something, even more than I could with some of my closer friends. That's gone. But our relationship will carry on, in my soul and in my spirit. There are still times when I address him. I know that at odd moments in my life Ian will be there. Not often, but occasionally. I'm certain he will be. And I feel that wherever he is, he's just fine.

KENNETH CHARLESON

I AN loved life and was not prepared to give it up without the very toughest of struggles. He was not a naturally combative or aggressive person, but he was very passionate about the things he believed in. He fought hard throughout his career to achieve excellence, and showed the same determination in the fight for his life.

I don't know how Ian coped with the knowledge of his illness. He found out that he was HIV positive as early as 1986. I was living abroad and looking back now, realize that we had precious little time with him in his hours of greatest travail. It was only a year before Ian died that my parents found out about his illness.

There was a period between 1986 and the beginning of 1989, when, as Ian later confessed to me, he lacked the enthusiasm and indeed the energy to work. He read scripts and then declined them, supposedly because he did not by then need to do just anything that was put in front of him.

But by the time he was fully in the grip of AIDS, he had recovered his nerve and sinew sufficiently well to cast off the lonely disguise of his illness and to move back into the spotlight of his life, his work and to resume the challenge of the stage.

The challenge he set himself was that of *Hamlet*.

We had a conversation one September evening in 1989. Ian was in the throes of rehearsing for the National Theatre's production of the play where he was to take on the role from Daniel Day Lewis. He was still, relatively speaking, well and strong, although his eyes and forehead were very puffed.

His eyes had become a major source of irritation to him. His constant complaint was that, as an actor, he could live with almost anything but the disfigurement of his face and partial loss of his sight.

This particular evening, his eyes were bad. They were slits in his head from which it was impossible to see either their colour or even the direction of his gaze. Here was a man about to step out onto one of the world's most important stages, in one of the world's most demanding stage roles, and he could not even see to eat without bending his head almost to the plate.

We had gone out for supper. Somewhere anonymous. Somewhere he would not be recognized.

The tables were close enough to have eaten off your neighbour's plate. It's funny how, even in such restrictive circumstances, you forget the proximity of total strangers and assume that they are far too busy with their own lives to be even remotely bothered with yours.

There we were, this odd couple, one in a pin-stripe suit and the other in jeans, T-shirt and dark glasses which he did not take off even in the subdued light of the small dining-room.

As Ian talked, it began to dawn on me just how close he felt to death, and yet how much he was still in control of his own destiny. He continued to pursue talk of the future and what he wanted to do next – after his eyes got better and his face resumed its normal appearance.

The second thing which struck me was how little I knew of his ambitions and what he wanted from life. Our adult lives did not have much in common. I began to wonder how much or how little I knew him.

There seemed to appear in front of me a patchwork of contrasting images of our lives: here and there; closeness and yawning distances; various little pieces of success and failure which brought us together and also kept us apart; our shared upbringing and love of music and the arts and yet the very different paths we had followed.

We enjoyed the same talents, the difference being that Ian had more of them than I. At times I was jealous, but predominantly I was proud of him. He could say it for all of us, mum, dad, Lizzie and I.

As children, both Ian and I were used to hearing my parents, particularly our mother, sing. We both had a pretty decent repertoire of popular songs by the time we were weaned. 'Lily Marlene', 'Heart of my Heart', 'Underneath the Arches' were easily rendered at a very early age.

One song which was to follow us through life, through any number and variety of situations, across national frontiers and past language, cultural and social barriers was Robert Burns' 'My Love is Like a Red, Red Rose'. Complete with kilts and angel faces Ian and I successfully offered up, heart and soul, with the purest tonal quality of boy sopranos, the unmatchable beauty of Burns' love poem, set to the most perfect of melodies. We would win the first prize of the evening wherever we happened to be. Nae problem tae the wee yins.

Edinburgh held our lives in its gently cupped hands. It is a city of many beautiful faces, of grace and style and elegance. It has remained remarkably unchanged in the forty-four years I have known it. It is Ian's final place of rest.

When Ian and I were quite small children, the family left Edinburgh for the more economically blessed south. It seemed to be at the other end of the earth but was in fact only the new town of Newton Aycliffe, near Durham. A small step for mankind but an enormous step for two wee jocks who spent the next couple of years defending their incomprehensibility behind a typically bluff, Scottish exterior and my agile fists and feet.

I remember seeming to spend the best part of three years, between the ages of five and eight, honing my skills as a fighting minority amongst a bunch of kids to whom Ian and I were both 'Scotty' as in 'Beam me up' but long before it was funny.

It was during one of the many confrontations between the two wee Scotties and a gang of local junior mafia, that stones began to fly. Ian and I hid behind an upturned wheelbarrow, the rest of the world out front held back only by the occasional handful of gravel and the odd half brick. Suddenly, Ian stood up and a flying missile, thrown carelessly, smacked him straight between the eyes, about an inch above his nose.

There was blood everywhere, a gnashing of teeth and instant panic among the juvenile delinquents. I grabbed Ian, stuffed a grubby handkerchief on his forehead to stem the bleeding and staggered fearfully home to paternal admonition and a reminder forever after that the resulting star-shaped scar might have been avoided if only . . .

In Newton Aycliffe we learned to build igloos in the drifting snow of a northern, country winter. That same winter we clambered aboard the Darlington bus on a Saturday heading for the market with all the other woolly hats and great coats, breath steaming out like smoke. I can remember the nest of shovels under the stairs; used to clear the great drifts of snow blown into dunes across the road.

In summer we would set off with holidaying grandparents in a very cramped Ford Prefect, off on a wonderful adventure, stopping on steep hills to disgorge all but the driver to push the hissing car up anything that was more than a one-in-ten incline.

Eventually we moved back to Edinburgh where the business of developing latent musical talent was to commence in earnest. My parents bought a piano, a substantial investment for them. It was an important acquisition, perhaps more so for Ian than for me for he had the greater talent. He carried his love of classical music unabated throughout his life. In later years, his greatest thrill was to see our sister Elizabeth succeed as a violinist and for her quartet, the Vanbrugh, to receive international recognition. The best thing is that from her, the best is yet to come.

As Ian and I grew into teenagers, music and the performing arts continued to play an important part in our lives, but from very different perspectives. By the time I was sixteen, I was playing in a rock band, whereas Ian aged sixteen was solo soprano with his school choir, performing on radio.

Our lives, therefore, had begun to diverge, except for one short but very significant period when they intertwined. That was at Edinburgh University in 1968 where I was a student of law, economics and accounting and Ian was in his second year of architecture. We were both involved in University DramSoc, Ian acting and I with the more prosaic task of raising money through programme advertising.

I call it significant now, because that was where Ian really discovered his desire to be an actor. He graduated in architecture and then threw it all in for the stage. Within two years of the DramSoc productions he enrolled at LAMDA and embarked upon his chosen career.

He devoted his life to his work both on and off the stage. In the end, he gave his life to the stage. His reawakened theatrical ambition would not let him take the easy path around his illness. He fought his illness through the medium of his art.

He chose to take on Hamlet when he knew his predicament was worsening. The sheer fire of his ambition and his belief in salvation through the part persuaded the director, Richard Eyre, against what might have been considered a common sense decision not to allow him to continue.

That evening, in that squashed-up, anonymous restaurant, Ian talked about his life and his ambitions and his decisions to take on Hamlet and to be the best at it. Not the best that he could be — that would be a lowly ambition — but the very best that there has ever been or would ever be.

He did not see it as the end, but as the first step towards a rehabilitation that he thought he owed himself. He went through the part as we ate, gesticulating direction with his fork, explaining what Shakespeare actually meant, explaining the play's historical context in a way I had not heard before and in a way which made me begin to understand *Hamlet* for the first time.

He cursed himself for a lapse in his own concentration in his career. He took his dark glasses off as he did so and carried on talking and gesticulating, ignoring the anxious stares of the diners around us at the grotesqueness of his appearance; not ignoring them so much as not recognizing them. And I in my growing elation forgot them too.

He still believed that his facial disfigurement might improve, but even if it didn't, so what? It would do, because the rest would be so compelling, so captivating, so energizing, so damn good, that he could walk out on stage with bandages around his face for all the difference it would make.

We believed that, he and I, in that restaurant that night, and he believed it when he walked out on stage on the first and every night he performed Hamlet. And it was true, it made no difference, because he believed so much in what he was doing and why he was doing it.

It was to be my last real conversation with him. It was probably the closest I had been to him for a long time. It served to emphasize the distance that had grown between us over years of going our different ways. But it also emphasized the fact that despite the gap, we were still brothers and loved each other for all that.

AIDS is a dreadful disease, not so much for what it is, but for what it does emotionally and psychologically to the sufferer and to those who love him or her.

We live in an age of science, although perhaps not in an age of reason. Science is pushing back the frontiers of knowledge at an ever increasing rate, but the communication of that knowledge is still slow.

Whatever age we happen to be in, however, there always falls to us, as human beings, the responsibility of compassion. If the 1990s is to be the age of conservation of nature, let us not forget the conservation of the human soul, upon which nature ultimately depends.

In his hour of greatest crisis, Ian gave everything he had to fight his illness and yet gave still more to achieve the greatest ever Hamlet. His spirit was wonderful to behold. Even in the extremes of suffering, the wildest of dreams can still be realized.

Ian was compassionate, generous and thoughtful. He was true

and gentle, and concerned about the human race. He was joyful and he could give that joy of life to anyone who needed it. He was a proper man.

Ian, of course, will always be here. Long after I'm gone, people will still watch *Chariots of Fire* and marvel at the actor who made the part his own just as those who were lucky enough to have seen it, will marvel at his Hamlet.

You carry all the universe around in you,
And all the generations of earth,
From time in the beginning, 'til time unto the end.
So shall it be, when com'st thou from thy midnight slumber,
Sailing through the night on seas of wisdom,
Far beyond the limits dreamt of, Dane, in thy philosophy.
Grasp thou this moment hard,
With fleshy hand around the stinging leaf,
And feel no pain, but feel the glory of thy union
With the universe and with the wisdom of the gods.

RICHARD EYRE

I didn't know Ian well until I worked with him on *Guys and Dolls* in 1982. I knew him then as an actor of charm, of wit, of skill, with a kind of engaging melancholy of the Mastroianni variety which he could dispel with a sardonic and self-mocking wit. He often looked truly beautiful, even angelic; then a mischievous smile would appear, and all thought of angels would fly away like frightened starlings.

I'd offered him a part in *Guys and Dolls* on the basis of his acting and hearing him sing at parties where he revealed a pure and wholly unaffected singing voice. It was typical of him that he insisted on singing the score for me before he accepted the part and equally typical that when he'd finished singing he said to me: 'You enjoyed that, didn't you, Richard?' He knew he could make an audience (and a director) cry with a romantic ballad, and he loved to do just that. As much as he loved to torment me with his relentless mockery of my attempts to learn to tapdance alongside the cast.

He was a fine, light, unfailingly truthful, romantic actor, something that the French value more than we do. Like Cary Grant, he had the gift of making the difficult look effortlessly simple. But with Brick in *Cat on a Hot Tin Roof* and with his Hamlet he discovered a new gravity in his work, a real weight and depth. He became, in my view, a heavyweight.

We had talked about two years ago about the parts that Ian desperately wanted to play, Richard II, Angelo, Benedick and Hamlet. (Even, as he said to me one day, 'Lear, God willing.') He had a real passion for Shakespeare, rather rare in his generation. He really loved the density of thought, the great Shakespearean paradoxes, the lyricism, the energy of the verse. He didn't want to paraphrase it; the meaning was for him in the poetry, and the poetry in the meaning.

When I asked him to play Hamlet, I knew that he'd been ill, had even had pneumonia, and that he still had a chronic sinus complaint which gave him large, swollen bags under his eyes. On bad days it was barely possible to glimpse the face beneath the swelling, a malicious parody of his beauty. He was without vanity, but not without hope. He told me that he was HIV positive and that he thought that the eyes would respond to treatment. When we embarked on rehearsals he was having regular, and immensely painful, acupuncture treatment and, later on, chemotherapy which exhausted and debilitated him. (Later in his illness he defiantly rejected all treatment; he wanted to be himself, however painful that was.)

About halfway through the rehearsal period we discussed the 'future', an unspecified projection. 'Do you think I can go on as Hamlet looking like this?' he said.

'You'll get better,' I said.

'We have to be positive,' he said. And we were. Our text was, of course, from *Hamlet*: 'There is nothing either good or bad but thinking makes it so.'

Hamlet is a poem of death. It charts one of the great human

[122]

rites of passage – from immaturity to accommodation with death. Hamlet grows up, in effect, to grow dead. Until he leaves for England ('From this time forth/My thoughts be bloody or be nothing worth') he is on a reckless helter-skelter swerving between reason and chaos. When he returns from England he is changed, 'aged', matured, reconciled somehow to his end. We see Hamlet in a graveyard obsessed with the physical consequences of death, and then, in a scene with Horatio, prior to the duel he talks about his premonitions of his end: '... thou wouldst not think how ill all's here about my heart. But it is no matter ... it is but foolery ... We defy augury. There is special providence in the fall of a sparrow. If it be now, 'tis not to come; if it be not to come, it will be now; if it be not now, yet it will come. The readiness is all. Since no man of aught he leaves knows aught, what is't to leave betimes? Let be.'

We talked a great deal about Hamlet's accommodation with death, always as a philosophical proposition, his own state lurking just below the surface, hidden subtext. Ian was very fastidious about the 'Let be.' It wasn't, for him, a chiding of Horatio, or a shrug of stoic indifference; it was an assertion, a proposed epitaph perhaps: don't fuss, don't panic, don't be afraid.

I've no idea if it was Kennedy's coinage, more likely one of his speechwriters, but the definition of courage as 'grace under pressure' was perfectly suited to Ian. It was something more than stoicism. He defied his illness with a spirit that was dazzling, quite without self-pity, self-dramatization, and, at least openly, despair. During rehearsals he was utterly without reserve. Where there had been a kind of detachment or caution, a 'Scottishness' perhaps, there was a deep well of generosity, of affection, a largeness of heart, and the only 'Scottish' characteristics that he showed were his doggedness and his persistence.

His last performance of *Hamlet* was less than eight weeks before he died and he acted as if he knew it was the last time he'd be on stage. He'd had flu and hadn't played the previous two nights; he was feeling guilt about what he saw as his lack of professionalism. 'If they pay you, you should turn up,' he said. His performance on that Monday night was, as Ian McKellen said, like watching a man who had been rehearsing for Hamlet all his life. He wasn't playing the part, he became it. By the end of the performance he was visibly exhausted, each line of his final scene painfully wrung from him, his farewell and the character's agonizingly merged. He stood at the curtain call like an exhausted boxer, battered by applause.

When he became unable to perform it was a real deprivation to him. Without that there was nothing to hang on to. 'You know me, Richard, if there are two people out there who I can impress I'd be there if I could.' And he would, if he'd had the strength. We're often accused of sentimentality in the theatre but it can't be sentimentality to miss terribly someone whose company gave so much joy, whose talent really *did* add to the sum of human happiness and whose courage was beyond admiration.

I had a letter from him just before Christmas. He said: 'One day when I'm better I've love to attempt Hamlet again and all the rest: and together we can revitalize Shakespeare. Anyway I hope this is not a dream and I can't tell you how much of a kick I got out of doing the part, if only for the short time I could . . .'

Let be.

IAN McKELLEN

As actors get old, their work is often enfeebled. Disappointed even embarrassed, we would rather they quietly retired and left us with memories of their maturity. So, those who knew only the public man, can be grateful that Ian Charleson's acting powers never declined and that, right at the end, he gave a performance which perhaps he could never have equalled.

When he played in *Bent,* for just one night in June 1989, was he testing himself for *Hamlet?* He was already ill and taking punishing medical treatment. His eyes were clearly swollen and he was risking gossip by appearing on-stage, although as Greta he was well disguised by make-up and costume. If his success that night, as the audience laughed and cheered, encouraged him to agree to do Hamlet, he knew that you can't disguise yourself in that part. Of all Shakespeare's challenges, Hamlet is the greatest. You ideally need voice and constitution in immaculate condition but you also need to commit your spirit, so that the audience finds itself assessing the actor's inner character as much as Hamlet's.

As a very young man, he had played Hamlet for the Cambridge

Theatre Company, but hadn't been happy with his performance. Hamlet was unfinished business. In the intervening years of success on-stage and on screen, he must have been half-hoping for a return engagement. Hoping too, after Sky Masterson and Tennessee Williams' Brick, that another hit at the National Theatre might properly establish him as a leading stage actor. When the chance came, even as his body was succumbing to the virus, he was determined to take it.

On Monday 13 November 1989, I was as apprehensive as any of his friends, that we might have to make allowances. He had not been strong enough to do every scheduled performance but he was determined to play that night, as the house would be full and many people he knew had tickets.

The Olivier can seem a beastly theatre for the actors. Its volume is too large for the size of the audience and, from the stage, you feel the need to shout and generally exaggerate, as you reach out to the 1100 people sitting yards and yards away. A very few experienced actors are at home there and none more so than Michael Bryant, who was playing Polonius. That night, Ian was his match. He never tried to shout. His voice was firm and sweet. The soliloquies are where Hamlet's generally fail but Ian spoke them like conversations on life and death, and shrank the vast auditorium to the intimacy of a drawing-room. That would have been remarkable under any circumstances but as his throat was physically distorted and his lungs impaired, we were witnessing a near miracle of will and energy.

Physically he was conserving his resources but so cunningly that it seemed exactly the performance he would have wanted to give had he been completely well. Only his eyes let him down. It's disheartening when the most expressive part of an actor's face is not working properly. But it genuinely didn't matter and

[128]

in some moments, as he stepped into shadow, we saw him beautiful as ever.

'O that this too too sullied flesh would melt,
Thaw and resolve itself into a dew.'

He covered his face with his thin, white hands. Hamlet was effortlessly aware of his own mortality and, without sentimentality or self pity, he made us all aware that young men, princes, actors – all of us – must die. Hamlet's journey to the fulfillment of the last scene, when he is ready to face his destiny, was clearly charted.

Most Hamlet's rush at the journey and the part itself. We display the angst, the bewilderment and the pain so forcefully, that we miss the character's everyday humanity. The revelation of the Charleson Hamlet was to show what he would have been like had he never met the ghost. We knew what he had been like at university, brightly and outrageously witty. It was obvious what a marvellously sympathetic friend he could have been and how easily Ophelia must have fallen for him. We believed her mourning 'that most noble and most sovereign reason', because we'd seen it for ourselves. He cracked jokes, not just the obvious impertinences to Polonius but in the final duel itself, where even the foils made us laugh.

It's not often, despite the plot, that Hamlet's intelligence is quite credible. Ian had a strong cast around him but he outthought them all.

In the green room afterwards, he was overwhelmed with praise and exceptional enthusiasm. He was hugging a bottle of champagne from an admiring theatre critic. Only when he got safely home did he give in to exhaustion. He didn't work again.

[129]

But he knew he'd been remarkably good and during his last eight weeks often talked about *Hamlet*, with a paperback script of it by his bed.